Bad Climber

Strappo

Warning- This book contains frequent episodes of alcoholic intoxication.

Front cover – Biblimotin, aka Ladyfinger 6000m, Pakistan.
Back cover – Photo Credit Simon Peck

Foreword - by Hector Padilla

In 1991, Boulder, Colorado was my playground, and climbing was my passion.

While searching for a partner to scale heights with, an office buddy pointed me towards a British transplant by the name of Roger Hughes, also known to his friends as 'Strappo,' a name that would soon become synonymous with adventure in my life. His quirky nickname intrigued me, and I was told that it might have been an abbreviation for the Italian word for overhanging, Strapiombante. I took it upon myself to do some fact checking and delved into an Italian dictionary and, sure enough, the name's origin did sound plausible. Maybe a reference to his prominent beer belly or the famous overhanging gritstone climb of the same name. Further research also revealed that Strappiombante, (with two p's) was an Italian word meaning, "Overwhelming." How hilarious! Now that truly seemed to fit the bill, based on some of the bizarre stories I'd heard about him.

Our first meeting was at a local bar where his eccentricity quickly surfaced. Strappo, ever the fashionably late entrant, greeted me not with a hello but with an unexpected declaration. "God, I hate partying," Over a couple of slowly sipped pints, we hit it off and made plans to climb the next day.

The morning rendezvous at his house was no less dramatic. As I approached, a toaster came hurtling out the door, soon followed by Strappo armed with a 9mm handgun. His frustration at the appliance's betrayal of his breakfast ended in a hail of bullets. "This bloody toaster will never burn my toast again," he proclaimed. And so began a future life of wild and spontaneous climbing adventures with this crazy, comedic villain.

Strappo was never one for the well-trodden paths. His spirit was nomadic, always in pursuit of uncharted pitches and serene, untraveled places. I was his willing companion, reaping the rewards of breathtaking and sometimes terrifying experiences. In those climbs, Strappo transformed from a mere acquaintance to my mentor and best friend.

Dedicated to a couple of awesome kids, Kashmir (left) and Summer. And to the mum that raised them well.

Contents

Chapter 1. Big Mistakes

Day-to-day life was often wearisome for my parents back in the late fifties and early sixties. My father, John Llewellyn Hughes produced glamorous artwork for magazines in the local printing shop, and like all loving mothers, Sylvia Joan Hughes scrimped, saved and shopped shrewdly to provide adequate meals and proper attire for my little baby sister; Jan and myself. We lived in a ramshackle, semi-detached house on Thorburn Road, Rock Ferry, Birkenhead, about one quarter mile from the oil slick beaches, rusted piers, and untreated sewage of the river Mersey estuary and only a short ferry ride over to the iconic city of Liverpool: four miles distant.

My dad loved to fish. Early childhood memories recall digging around the tideline with a bucket and spade in search of evil looking bait worms called lugworm and ragworm that fish seemed to adore. Our beach casting fishing rods were over twice my size and after a little practice, I found I could hurl those baited hooks and lead weights enormous distances, out into the grey and oftentimes fog enshrouded waters below the promenade sea wall near our house. We would reel in mostly bottom feeding flat fish like plaice, dab and sole and devoured everything that we caught with great relish around a lively dinner table. These were happy times for the very young me back then. Doing my homework on the rug in front of a roaring coal fire, night times in bed with a rubber hot water bottle tucked between my legs to keep the cold at bay, occasional trips to the pub with my mum and dad and an endless array of American tv sit coms, soccer, and horse racing, on our two-channel black and white television.

Over the years, our lot improved considerably. Better employment for my dad meant living in a nicer house in a more upscale neighborhood. Uppingham Road in Wallasey was tree lined and very serene, with the distant church bells ringing out the time every fifteen minutes and best of all, there was a huge playing field at the bottom of the road.

I think I was around eight years old when my mum and dad started brewing their own beer and wine. Our house suddenly became the social hub of the area with neighbors 'just popping by.' Jugs of the recently fermented liquids flowed, and evenings of loud, raucous laughter ensued. I was no stranger to alcohol. A photo in our family album showed me being bottle fed Guinness at the tender age of six days old by my dad. Whether the photo was faked or not I will never know, but I acquired a taste for stout beer very quickly in later years.

My schooling was going reasonably well around that time. I loved art and was very creative; always getting good grades. I would make top of the class in English on more than one occasion but generally came bottom of the class in mathematics and science subjects which I just couldn't fathom and so therefore loathed and hated. The primary school that I attended was very conformist and deeply religious, which I chose to completely disregard, even at such a young age. Despite all this, I still really enjoyed going to school. That is until one particular day changed my whole life around, irrevocably, and completely, forever.

The eleven plus standardized IQ examination was administered to students in their final year of primary education, the outcome of which would largely determine what type of future schooling they might receive. At age 11 or 12 years old, a pupil's entire future life would hinge upon the success or failure of this one exam. There was also evidence of class bias. Grammar schools were largely attended by middle class children while working class children ended up in Secondary schools.

I flunked the math and failed the test outright.

And so, in 1966, at the very tender age of eleven, I was demoted down, and shipped off to Saint Georges Secondary Modern, a school for social rejects and the drastically under-privileged, the rebels and those who, for whatever reason, were not deemed to be going anywhere special in life. Like a train suddenly changing tracks, my behavior changed almost overnight, going from a shy, retiring, and meek kid to a mother's worst nightmare. In the ensuing years, I followed the time-worn doctrines of my peers; gang-fighting, being bullied by older kids, bullying new kids, insatiable kleptomania, and vandalism. Then one day, the whole archaic school system changed on me and the Eleven plus exam was deemed unjust. By the time I was transferred back to a real (Grammar) school again, the damage had already been done, for now I hated school with such a degree of vengeful loathing. This fluffy modern school seemed so tame by comparison and did nothing to appease my perpetual craving for getting into trouble. As with most of the British, I discovered alcohol at a very early age. It came during another tedious, life-changing examination: the Certificate of Secondary Education exams. These CSE's were a precursor to higher level exams which would ultimately allow access to higher level college or university education.

The year was 1971. My beautiful watercolor art paper was close to completion. The shadow cast from a rustic stone bridge upon the shimmering waters below cast a perfect interplay of ochre and deep charcoal. I felt warm with pride, and smug with anticipation of a decent grade. The lunchtime bell rang and my two skinhead partners; Paul and Degsy, invited me to join them in the nearby park for a much-needed diversion. It was peaceful here and must have just rained, for the air was cool, and a solemn mist lingered above the lake to hush away the distant drone of brawling traffic from out beyond the woodlands.

The powerful silence was rudely awakened by the shrill scrape of Doctor Martin boots as we arrived abruptly and breathlessly before the park bench. We flung ourselves down and without the slightest spoken word, proceeded to rip the caps off our bottles of strong apple cider and began chugging in earnest. Our lunchtime hour of mayhem was fleeting. Objects quickly became distorted and vision blurry, as we careened across the park; over bushes and through hedgerows in a heroic attempt to make it back to school in time for the afternoon lessons.

We parted company at the school gate, and I set a course for the Arts building in a kind of tacking, pinball swagger across the playground to rejoin my classmates.

Desperately clutching the doorframe, I leered drunkenly into the classroom. My friends were already hard at work, putting the finishing touches to their paintings.

After regaining my seat, the fumbling began in earnest. "Oh god, I've really done it this time," I groaned inwardly. The fattest paintbrush was by far the easiest to use, so beginning in the top right-hand corner, I began to topcoat my masterpiece in watery, black paint. Halfway down the paper, the master's stroke was added with gusto as the inevitable catastrophe struck. The brush suddenly jerked to the floor as my head recoiled from the sleek power jet of liquid vomit launched from a distended throat.

"U-ugh," I drooled, as I raised my slimed chin in time to catch the manic howls and shrieks of my classmates. My 'top shelf tsunami' had surged across the one large table and captured at least two other paintings, sweeping them unceremoniously onto the floor.

Schooling really took a back seat after that performance. Not that this mattered any more, because while on a hunting and gathering foray at our local bookstore, I had coveted an instructional book on how to rock climb. Learning to lead rock climbing routes by first reading a book might be viewed as pure suicide by many, indeed, I would never have wished that trial upon even my worst enemies. There were so many critical elements: Tying into the rope, belaying, taking the risks of leading while placing adequate protection. Practicing all these skills became a fearful progression, one fraught with many unseen dangers. On a path with too many potentially fatal errors to make, having to learn from those mistakes; yet not being allowed to make just one was tough. Sadly, we had no-one to watch over our every move, or ingrain vital safety procedures into our thick, adolescent skulls. At that stubborn age of naïve stupidity, learning the hard way seemed like the sole option. Climbing offered a chance to put all that untested bravery up on the witness stand. Failing on a climb would rarely invoke castigation from others. That special feeling of worthlessness would now come from deep within. Suddenly, all our previous juvenile antics seemed childishly immature, embarrassing, and hollow.

All criminal activities ceased forthwith, and a menial, low-paying job was acquired to finance this incredible new passion. In five teenage years, the transformation had gone from a meek little boy; to mindless thug; to impassioned climbing novice. It was like leaving the farm roads and suddenly joining the Interstate. And on that road, I was now irrevocably set. One time-worn, life-long question still nagged though: begging a truthful response. Was risk taking already ingrained in my bloodline or was it just pure luck? Could perpetual adrenaline addiction be blamed on ancient warrior genes? Unlikely. Perhaps this fortunate outcome rested solely upon a simple off day at school and the distant byproduct of unforeseen circumstances? Had I not discovered rock climbing, I could have easily ended up in a thankless, mundane life, perhaps in jail or worse? This was a time in my life to just accept what had happened and to be extremely thankful.

My best friend at the time was known to his friends as 'Bike Chain.' He was none too sissy of a character; having been named after his favorite weapon of intimidation. Any enemies that he might have had were probably in luck thanks to his sudden redirection of energy into something other than fighting.

In an urban sprawl of pre-war housing, an abandoned, tree-filled quarry had been our playground since childhood days. Known as The Breck, it was a stomping ground for scruffy gangs of snot-nosed kids, whose main mission in life seemed to be terrorizing other, smaller kids. The red sandstone quarry sat on a small hill and overlooked the main town of Wallasey. It was hemmed in on three sides by rows of red-brick, semi-detached houses whose back gardens overlooked the tops of these walls. Despite their liberal coating of graffiti, these outcroppings of short, pocketed sandstone were ideal for the latest brand of fun and games. It was a sanctuary; a place to wile away every available hour; at weekends and after school during the warm, sultry evenings of early summer.

On one such evening, Bike Chain and I hunkered down beneath the overhanging wall in the back of the quarry; eagerly leafing through our well-thumbed climbing instruction manual. A few days earlier, we had traversed the whole buttress by standing in stirrups and placing a string of thin, soft steel pitons[*] into horizontal seams near the top of the wall. I had led the first section into the middle of the highest, blankest place and then anchored myself in. As Bike Chain inched his way slowly towards me, he tapped the pitons back out with his hammer. I would take in the slack rope between us and brace myself for a fall; should one of his pitons suddenly pop out on him.

A sharp yell from below had me startled. It was the uniformed Park Keeper; yelling at us to come down; or he'll call the police. We completely ignored him, for we had no choice; being so engrossed in completing the fearful journey across the severely overhanging face without any serious accident. By many strokes of incredible luck, we made it across to flat ground just before dark. The Park Keeper had long since wearied of our

---

[*] Pitons, aka pins, are metal spikes driven into the rock and used for protection and aid.

antics and left for his dinner. Mercifully, no cops had ever been called.

In surviving this day, we had mastered the most complex chapter in the book; a highly advanced series of techniques known collectively as 'aid climbing.' This was like sprinting long before learning to crawl; but with our bookworm method of mastering the sport, every chapter in the book seemed worthy of equal significance. Now we would tempt fate once again by following the explicit directions in chapter five. This would be the original, 'classic' style of roped descent technique known as abseiling, or rappelling. It is a very outdated method because it relies only on painful body friction instead of using a friction brake and a harness. The rope runs down between the legs, around one hip and then back over the shoulder instead. I conducted a final check, but everything appeared satisfactory as I prepared to kick away from the railings at the top of the overhanging wall. My descent was going well and soon I was gently spinning in space, well out from the rock. With lousy neck protection, the rope began to grind into my jugular like cheese wire. Not wishing to be decapitated at such an early stage in my climbing career, I committed a most appalling error by grabbing at my collar with my crucial brake hand, thus allowing the rope to whip off my shoulder and slide down to my elbow. In the same heartbeat, it flipped off my side and up to the back of my knee. Somehow, I ended up dangling twenty feet off the ground, with the rope cinched firmly around just one elbow. With all feeling lost in my forearm, extreme panic took over and I screamed at Bike Chain to run up to the anchor and chop the rope with our hammer, allowing me to crash to the ground. As Bike Chain's repeated blows began to mash the rope up top, I suddenly remembered another technique that I had read about in the book but never tried. It was a technique called prussiking; whereby a thinner sling is looped twice around the main rope and then threaded back through itself. The 'prussik' knot will slide up a fixed rope but locks off when weighted, allowing the climber to progress slowly upwards.

In blind desperation, I rigged the knot as per the book's illustration, and then stepped up into a sling. This released my body weight from the lifeless forearm and allowed me to shuffle back down to the ground. This hitherto untried technique had saved my arm and probably some major leg bones from serious breakage as well. The epic drama should have prompted us to quit climbing and divert our energies elsewhere, but in fact, quite the reverse happened. I had averted a serious accident only through memorization of a certain knot. Still, this event gave me the confidence I needed to conjure up delusions of total immortality. Acting on these false assumptions, we scrounged up a canvas army tent and the barest essentials and boarded a bus for a weekend among the mountain crags of North Wales. Without maps, guidebooks, or any other clues as to a viable destination, we vacated the bus at the first glimpse of a jagged hillside. Luckily, we'd been set down in the tranquil, sheep-infested hamlet of Capel Curig. Quite soon, waves of drizzle moved in, and we quickly started to feel a little out of our element but solved this dilemma by marching over to a nearby farmhouse and begging the farmer for a place to camp. For a very nominal fee we were escorted to the back of a nearby field and instructed to pitch our tent behind a dry-stone wall. There was a climbing and backpacking store in the village too, so we tracked down the relevant guidebook and absorbed some key data.

The next morning, a leisurely hitchhike took us to a mountainous, steep-sided valley known as Cwm Idwal. It was a forbidding place, with even stouter cliffs littering its distant peaks. As we followed the well-worn trail, violent gusts of wind tore at our clothing and churned the lake water into a frenzy of white-capped waves.

The scale of these mountains was completely deceptive to us. From a distance, the Idwal slabs appeared to blend into a more dramatic sweep of grey rock that rose up into the swirling clouds. Although none too steep or technically demanding, most of the named routes on the slabs terminated at a grassy ledge that was almost five hundred feet above the ground. We would need to follow our route description carefully so as to locate the safest stopping places. It was not only the immensity of our venture that daunted us. Other nearby climbers seemed to be much better equipped and sported brightly colored clothing and actual helmets. The various climbing calls that echoed about the cliffs exuded an air of proficiency and competence that we did not share. We began to feel thoroughly dwarfed by our bumbling lack of experience. Sporadic bouts of drizzle coated the rock with a slippery film of moisture, but inviting twin cracks departed the ground, affording easy moves and some reassuring protection. I clambered up these initial cracks with little thought to style, so absorbed was I in a mission to quickly gain height. As people on the ground faded to become mere abstract scenery, my new-found confidence died when the friendly cracks began to fizzle out. There were other solid cracks that beckoned, but to get to them I would have to traverse sideways for about fifteen feet.

"Watch me here," I called down to Bike Chain.

Stepping away from my cozy niche, I began teetering rightwards across the thin slab. In a flash, my foot skidded out of the greasy pocket, and I bounced back down the cliff with ever increasing speed.

Astoundingly, I ground to a painful halt only a short distance above my fear-stricken partner on the ground. My ribs ached from the rope tied around my waist.

While counting the bruises on my hips and elbows, I realized that my momentum had ripped out three pieces of protection on the way down. This new level of incompetence made my previous rappel accident at the Breck seem incredibly tame by comparison.

Soon however, the sun began to shine through and added a few strokes of color to a bleak, grey landscape. Even the glistening slabs dried off and became an object of desire again.

We returned to the fray and followed another party of climbers up the easier and more continuous crack systems further right. With a perfect balance of elation and apprehension, we managed to climb almost five hundred feet of moderate slabs without any further mishaps or injury.

Once again, our raging incompetence only served to add spice to the daunting process of learning to climb rock. For the next six months, the Friday night bus would whisk us back to these uncompromising and windswept crags. No adversity could stifle the craving to pit our skills against such a challenging place as this. As the seasons changed, we became a little fitter, but no less dim-witted as we adopted the habit of carrying every scrap of heavy camping and climbing gear with us wherever we'd go. Classic ridge scrambles landed us at mountain summits that would seem to live forever above the clouds. When rare bouts of drier weather allowed, we would pitch the tent below a particular cliff and wage our war of ascent upon a host of fine climbs.

Autumn brought with it shorter days and much colder nights. We endured a string of truly miserable ordeals as gale force winds raged on and off for a whole month.

Our adventures culminated in nothing more than soggy sleeping bags and bitterly cold, sleepless nights. The flimsy tent leaked like a sieve and as the rain flooded in, we would bale pools of rainwater from the tent floor with a saucepan while holding up the collapsing walls with our freezing backs.

Morale soon reached an all-time low.

Having just spent two solid days engaged in this unsavory pursuit, Bike Chain and I were finally ready to throw in the towel and let our attentions drift elsewhere.

But as we cowered in the doorway of Capel Curig's grocery store on a dark, rainy Sunday evening two other climbers approached. They were also waiting for the same bus back towards Liverpool. We chatted amicably and they informed us that they were members of a climbing club that met in a local pub in our town every Wednesday night. They invited us to come along and meet everyone. This we did and suddenly, like-minded people were driving us out to Wales. From here on, we shacked up in a warm hostel and began to benefit from the encouragement and guidance from other, more qualified climbers. Our climbing improved in leaps and bounds. Not only did we begin tackling harder graded climbs, but at the same time, started to become dimly aware of our limitations, being less inclined to act like cretins and jump in way over our heads. In doing so, we began to enjoy ourselves for once.

At one of the beer-swilling club meets some months later, it was announced that there would be an organized trip to Chamonix, in the French Alps in the upcoming summer months. Wide-eyed and incredulous, Bike Chain and I were in awe at the possibilities and signed up immediately. This caused a minor rift with some of the senior club members. A few of the more experienced alpinists in the group were dead against unleashing two complete novices upon such a hazardous environment. Others saw this as an overreaction and were of the opinion that we should just wade in and try to learn by our mistakes.

This 'discussion' was never really resolved and resurfaced again at Snell's campground, one week after arriving in Chamonix. The weather had been uncooperative and all we'd accomplished thus far were a couple of overnight visits to some high mountain huts.

Then a high-pressure system arrived, bringing with it cold but clear days. Bike Chain and I, aka 'Team bumbly' had decided to attempt the serious North Face of the Col Du Plan as our very first alpine experience. I had already fallen into two crevasses while crossing glaciers en route to visiting the huts. We hadn't read anything about glacier travel and had no clue that climbers were supposed to rope up as a safeguard against such a disaster. Luckily, I had stopped short at the armpits and could be dragged out of the crevasse by the scruff of the neck. Peering into the icy blue depths where my feet had just dangled should have been a strict warning though; but alas; stupidity still prevailed.

We packed our newly acquired ice climbing gear, sleeping bags and some food and caught the evening cable car up to below the snow line. As we bedded down for the night out on the open talus fields below the face, we traced our proposed climb up the many hanging snowfields, interspersed by ridges of rock.

It looked like a suicidally dangerous venture to us but having recently been in the epicenter of that heated debate; one in which our abilities had been called into question, neither of us would give the slightest thought to backing down. Of course, we could never admit to any fear or doubt to each other either, and so we both drifted off to sleep that night with extreme trepidation.

The next morning, we strapped on crampons[*] and scrunched up four hundred feet of ice to a narrow platform next to the bergschrund. This gaping crevasse marked the point where the glacier met the steeper north face above and we actually displayed a modicum of common sense by breaking out the rope and tying into it.

The minutes drifted by as Bike Chain peered uneasily into the blue green depths of the chasm. Suddenly spurred into action, he stepped back and then vaulted to the other side, landing in the softer snow above. The rope lay uselessly strewn about my feet, but after Bike Chain kicked out a standing place in the slope, he pulled up the slack rope and belayed me up. Had we even thought to seek out a safe belay, we probably would not have found one, for as I energetically kicked a series of deep footsteps up the slope above, the snow began to

---

[*] a series of metal spikes, usually twelve, which are strapped to the soles of mountaineering boots to drastically improve purchase on snow and ice.

thin down and soon I was making contact with the blank rock underneath. Every time I tried to step up, the snow collapsed under my weight, and I slithered further back down than before. A hundred feet below me the gaping blue mouth of the bergschrund instilled sheer terror in me. I suddenly saw every reason to get far away from this evil place as possible, and began to pick my way carefully downwards, bounding back across the large crevasse and onto the relative safety of the ice-ledge beyond.

The whole experience had left us both a little shaken. It was dangerous and very insecure work, 'and we wanted nothing more to do with it.

Bike Chain set off down the icy slope below the platform but made the mistake of facing outwards instead of sidestepping and plodded downhill with his axe dangling uselessly by his side.

We were still tied together though, and I fed the rope out to him, but only through the fingers of one hand. Suddenly, his heels skidded out from underneath him, and he instantly began to tumble down the icy slope at high speed. He quickly regained control by rolling back over and braking with the tip of his axe. Meanwhile, the rope had been whipping through my burning fingers as I tried but failed to check his rapid descent. After a heated exchange of words, Bike Chain picked himself up and continued downwards, facing outwards once again!

He slipped a second time and I watched with complete horror, as events unfolded in the blink of an eye yet seemed to hang in time, like a slow-motion action replay.

I turned and watched as the remainder of the rope snaked off the ledge. With less than a few seconds to act, I swung around and embedded my axe into the ice next to me in a desperate act of blind reflex. Had my wrist been inside the ice axe strap, I might have lost that hand, because at that same moment, I was whisked off into space; dragged to my death by my incompetent partner. Having just thrown away my axe; I now had no hope of controlling the fall and hurtled down the ice at ever-increasing speed on a fatal collision course with boulders and other avalanche debris down below.

Repugnance of my impending death was cut short as I was suddenly brought to lung-crushing halt by the rope. Bike Chain had watched me come tumbling down after him and had the presence of mind to wrap a few loops around the shaft, sink his axe into the slope and throw his full body weight on top of it. Miraculously, the hickory wooden handle of his ice axe had just withstood the impact of a three-hundred-foot fall. Our drama had gone from a life-taking to a life-saving experience; and all in a matter of mere seconds.

While not fully conscious, I managed to get stood up on the slope, then noticed a steady trickle of blood seeping from out of my sleeve. I had torn the skin clean off my right elbow and could no longer use that arm. I felt little or no pain, only the tremendous relief of having survived yet another incredibly close call.

There are a lot fewer 'I told you so's,' uttered when we stumbled sheepishly back into camp and recounted the tale of my near-death experience to the rest of the crew. However, Bike Chain's conscience began to steer him away from climbing after he so nearly dragged me to my death. Guilt, humiliation, and a fondness for fighting prompted him to quit the sport right there and then and return home to join the British Army.

Dave 'Bike Chain' Smalley was gone. We would never see each other again.

Having narrowly survived my own 'trial by fire' by teaching myself to climb, my analytical brain deemed me ready for more risk-induced adrenalin and endorphin release. As I began my own journey home for urgent medical treatment on my elbow, climbing in every remote corner of the world had simply become my one sole obsession. I started to conjure up unshakeable fantasies of tackling vertical granite walls tucked away in remote corners of the world. All the most recent fears had faded away and unquestioning optimism had once again reared it's ugly head.

Above the town, a chaotic jumble of jagged peaks and glaciers enticed with the pink afterglow of a spectacular alpine sunset and as the evening train gathered momentum, drawing me away from twinkling lights of Chamonix, I was already lost in thought.

Perhaps I'd fare better elsewhere, I mused.

It would take seven more years of hit and miss climbing adventures before I would find myself ready for the giant leap into the realm of multi day big wall climbing.

Chapter 2. Pussball

"Desires fulfilled breed more desires." ~Sri Nisargadatta Maharaj~

The infamous Snell's campsite on the outskirts of Chamonix had been a righteous stomping ground for infection and disease. No bathrooms, just a bleak mud-soaked field set amid a pine forested minefield alive with dollops of fetid human waste flagged with encrusted toilet paper.

The flies loved it. They also loved my pus encrusted elbow too. By the time I arrived back in my hometown of Wallasey two days later, my badly infected wound was in critical need of a painful deep cleaning and strong antibiotics. As a healthier scab reformed, I returned to my work as a printing machine operator, arguably one of the most boring professions on the planet, but the price I had to pay for opting out of higher education at only age sixteen to start this tedious four-year apprenticeship.

While climbing the three flights of stairs to the dreaded printing press on Monday mornings, my mind would switch back into autopilot zombie mode, only to be reawakened by the five o'clock bell. My precious weekends in the mountains became my savior and the sole focus in my life. The piss poor weekly wage did allow me to purchase some much-needed climbing gear though, with a little cash left over to splurge on Wednesday night Gwydyr club meets at the Park Hotel and weekend climbing trips to our climbing hut, a renovated chapel near Capel Curig in North Wales.

The Gwydyr Mountain Club members (pronounced Gwi-theer) were an ever-increasing circle of social miscreants and larger-than-life characters, all sharing a passion for weekend mountain hikes or days at the crag. After the recent loss of Bike Chain, I was keen to cement new ties with likeminded climbing partners. Over the coming months, a rebellious rabble rose from the ranks.

Leigh McGinley was a very talented athlete who had recently competed in the triple jump for his school against future legend and three-time gold medalist, Keith Connor. When Leigh had discovered rock climbing and had then decided to spend all his Saturdays in the mountains instead of on the school racetrack, his bullying headmaster had threatened to withhold his crucial exam results. The resulting uproar between the school and his parents bestowed on him the same exact loathing for academics as I had felt. When we first met, he recounted the tale of what had happened the night before this crucial competition. Apparently, he had triple jumped in his sleep and had vaulted out of the bedroom window and into the garden. He was staying the night as a guest with an unknown family and had to wake them all up in the wee hours, clad only in his underwear!

Tom Jones won the nickname 'Stick Insect' for his lanky, breadstickesque appearance. With an ideal climbing frame, 'Sticko', like Leigh, was destined to become an adept and dedicated climber in years to come.

The list of newcomers kept growing, along with an array of bizarre nicknames. Leigh became Manwel. Tim Carruthers became Squint. Phil Moore became Clint. Our newly formed gang spent all available evenings bouldering on the high friction, pocketed red sandstone walls of The Breck. This was the scene of my nearly catastrophic rappelling accident two years earlier.

Another Gwydyr club member at the forefront at this time was Chris Hall (aka Pussball). He was a was a Valvoline oil engineer, stocky, with a bushy beard and a very animated soul, he gave off a slightly gnomelike appearance. We hit it off immediately and as we chatted amicably in the Gwydyr's private room upstairs from the lounge bar of the Park Hotel, pint followed pint followed by more pints. Our conversation grew in fervor and decibels. Then John Huxley, our club president stood up and made the announcement. It was revealed that another club foray to the French alps was being planned for the coming summer. The memory of my near fatal fall was completely absent as Pussball and I began to scour the guidebooks for a suitable alpine route to test ourselves on, finally opting for a pure rock-climbing classic. The 800-foot, sun baked, south facing, Rebuffat route on the Aiguille Du Midi is situated below the cable car station atop the Midi's precipitous summit. The route offers roughly nine rope lengths of technical climbing. The estimated guidebook time for this route was three to five hours. Our forthcoming epic would take us a grueling fourteen!

The scale and complexity of the face became apparent to us as we kicked steps down and around the final short section of glacier and hopped onto a large grey rock ledge below the face. It was a morning of perfect sunshine and complete solitude as we sat breathless, trying in vain to absorb the vast panorama of distant peaks, knife edged ridges and glaciers that had unfolded before us. We began to dress in climbing regalia, stuffing our boots and crampons into our one single climbing backpack, along with some warmer clothes, chocolate bars and a little water.

We had trained hard for this long sought-after route, bagging a healthy tick list of classic mid-range climbs around the crags in Wales, the Lake District, the Peak and even Southwest England. I felt confident that our new level of technical competence would measure up to what lay ahead for us.

We gained height rapidly, despite the ungainly pack carried by the second climber. The second pitch, an ever sweeping 'S' shaped finger crack had been heralded as one of the best single pitches in the entire Chamonix region.

I arrived at the small ledge above that crack with shrieks of elation. This was indeed the best pitch I had ever been on.

Pussball and I continued to swap leads as we continued up corner and flake systems, making decent time and savoring every moment of the climb, despite a growing apprehension, as the glacier below us receded into the distance. This was by far the longest climb we had ever been on, that, coupled with the yawning exposure below our feet gave rise to some tense moments. It was now late in the afternoon, and we still hadn't seen another soul on the route, which amazed us. Just the occasional tiny pin prick specks of skiers down on the Valle Blanche glacier far below.

Soon we could sense that the final summit spire was close at hand, but suddenly, route finding became very uncertain and a cause for some heated debate. Nothing related to the tattered guidebook page that I had stuffed in my top pocket.

From our exposed belay there looked to be three choices available to us. Shooting up and leftwards was an alluring hand crack that disappeared into unseen terrain. Straight above was a repulsive wide crack snaking up through overhangs that bristled with ancient wooden wedges replete with rotting pieces of webbing, while off to the right lay a snow filled gully, also leading us up into God knows where. After a little head scratching, we both agreed that the left-hand crack might be the best option.

Pussball launched upwards, punching in solid hand jams in the crack until the rope stopped moving and a long pause ensued.

"How's it going up there?" I ventured, after what seemed like an age of inactivity and the onset of real panic down in the ranks. "I'm stuck. The crack has ended, and I just don't know what to do next," his voice trembled. More time drifted by as the rope inched up, then back down in my hands.

"Hey Strappo, there's a wire cable dangling down from the cable car station off to my left." "Yeah, I see it." There was indeed a solitary thin metal cable draped down the face off to our left. I hadn't paid much attention to it, focused as I was on Pussball's antics above. "I really need help! Why don't you tie off the lead rope to the belay and free solo over to the wire and try to flick it over to me so that I can try and climb it."

The whole notion seemed so unthinkable, so absurd; but would it actually work? In blind desperation I decided to give it a try. Tying the lead line securely into the anchor I surveyed the distance between me and the wire, perhaps thirty feet of what might be difficult terrain, then a peek at the terrifying exposure below. With a long, deep breath and a thundering heart, I untied from the belay and launched into the traverse, blindly feeling out the moves and praying not to pass a point of no return. Soon enough the wire loomed in front of me. Then another thought occurred to me. What if it was electrified? What if it was some errant wire that was part of the system used to power the cable cars above us? How utterly lamentable, that I might get zapped, my cranium exploding like a glob of molten lava as I'd go cartwheeling back down the face like a discarded sack of glowing embers.

With few other options available to me I made the call, cautiously at first, finger tapping it quickly and lightly, then more deliberately, then feeling a sudden flood of relief as no searing pain or shower of sparks hit me. Greatly relieved, I grabbed hold of a solid chunk of granite at face level with one hand and then grasped the cable with the other and after a few sweeping tries managed to flick the wire over to Pussball, who was still perched, gargoyle like, eighty feet above me. With adrenaline now peaking I teetered back to my belay station and tied back in.

Things were getting quite desperate. We were making risky choices and losing control of the situation. As I gazed nervously skywards, Pussball proceeded to attempt a hand over hand up the cable like a deranged batman, only to slither back to his highest piece of protection and hang on the rope again. Yelling with frustration, he tried again, then again, with the same result. Our assumed safety net of confidence and competence was unravelling.

The prussik knot was next. This was the knot that had saved my forearm during my moronic rappelling accident years earlier.

Now frantic, Pussball wrapped a sling around the wire three times, looped it back through itself then slid the knot up the wire. Next, he fashioned a foot loop with two slings tied together and then clipped into the knot before stepping up. The knot slid effortlessly back down the wire and Pussball screamed more obscenities.

"Nothing is working. "Screw this, I'm coming down," he wailed. Luckily his highest protection piece was bombproof so without further ado I lowered him back to my belay ledge from this single point as he removed all remaining protection from the crack.

Then, as we both heaved on one end of the rope to retrieve it, a small twist in the other end lodged in a constriction thirty feet up and jammed the rope fast.

We couldn't believe this was really happening to us. We started to contemplate the notion of seeking some kind of assistance. But from whom?

Down on the glacier far below us we spied a group of maybe five or six skiers, elegantly carving turns down the Valle Blanche below. With nothing more than just a mutual nod we started yelling for help at the top of our voices.

With what started out as "Help! Help," soon turned into an attempt to convey the same in French.

"Attention !! Je suis très fatigue,"

which roughly translated to:

"Can I get your attention down there! I am very tired!!"

The skiers stopped and gazed back up at us, mere specks high on the wall, I imagine they probably cracked some very funny jokes before continuing with their day, as we looked on with abject dismay.

After a moment's silence, Pussball tied back into the remaining rope and scurried back up the crack, deftly freeing the jammed end, retying back in and lowering back down to the ledge. Soon we were reunited with all our rope and another chance to keep pushing on.

It was getting late now. The granite around us glowed a reddish bronze in the clear light of late afternoon.

The snowy, right-hand gully was really our only other option, so I set off warily into the gully and began punching and kicking steps and holds in the soft, wet snow, quickly gaining height. Skirting some loose blocks I landed abruptly at the shoulder of the mountain, directly below the final bayonet shaped summit needle. Although still completely lost, I was relieved to come across some anchor pitons festooned in old rope slings. Soon, both Pussball and I were assembled at the shoulder with no clear notion of what to do next. We were peering down the Aiguille du Midi's north side, a frigid, icy wall dropping down into the gully below.

Then suddenly we both noticed the other climber. He was at the top of the gully, leaning on a metal railing and clad in a thick red down jacket. His hands were cupped around a mug of something warm.

"Hello over there. I think we're off route. How do we get out of here?"

From 300 yards away, our friend yelled back the crucial information that we so desperately needed, his voice echoing back through the gloom of late evening.

We would rappel down the north wall below us. First a short forty foot one, then a longer rappel down into the base of the icy gully below, then we'd have to climb up that gully to the cable car station tunnels, and safety. It all looked very unappealing.

I went first, using the same classic technique I had used at the Breck fiasco when first learning to climb. You would straddle the rope between the legs, bring it back around the hip and over the opposite shoulder, with a final loop around your forearm behind you.

The terrain was mixed and steep. In no time at all I'd landed at a broad ledge with another set of anchors, clipped in and yelled for Pussball to come down next.

Suddenly another drama came into play when, about half-way down, the rope somehow slipped off his shoulder and he flipped backwards, just as the rope slipped from his hip to up behind his knee. I looked on in abject horror as a much more serious replay of my own, exact mishap unfolded before me. All hunched up and clutching the rope with a terrified grip, he clung on and slithered downwards, as the rope gouged deepening grooves into his fingers. Pussball was seconds away from losing his grip and falling to his death. Then right above the belay ledge he did cut loose from the rope, but I had him. Leaning at full stretch out from the belay I had a firm hold on the slings draped around his neck and shoulders. He bounced unceremoniously onto the ledge and stopped.

Wincing with pain, he informed me that, with severe rope burns on his inside finger knuckles, he had just lost the use of both hands.

And we still had to get down the longer rappel and then ascend the icy gully below.

Belay devices of any kind had not yet been invented in the early 1970's. The lead climber's very life depended upon a simple waist belay. In the event of a fall, the belayer would lock off the rope with the 'brake forearm' shoved tightly across his lower chest. This was how I would have to get him down. With friction from the rope around my waist and then around both forearms, I began lowering Pussball down the wall. He was a whole lot of dead weight though, and as my woolen gloves failed to check his rate of descent, he began to speed up, finally landing in the gully with a resounding thump amid the clatter of dislodged rocks.

Nightfall was close at hand as I arrived next to him. With safety only a couple of hundred feet away I rearranged the rack of climbing gear and in a complete frenzy, launched up the mixed rock and ice above, fully aware that I was now free soloing. Pussball would be unable to stop me should I slip and fall. Soon enough the railing came into sight and then the joyous disbelief that I was actually clipping into it! A flood of wild emotions; extreme relief that we had skirted a string of very close calls. Within those moments of pure clarity came a sudden, solemn resolve to quit all this alpine climbing crap for good. Find something I was good at. This resolve became even more unshakeable as I hand winched poor Pussball up that wretched gully to safety in almost total darkness.

We bade the French alps farewell and scurried back to England with our tails wedged firmly beneath our recently shrunken ball sacks.

Getting back to a routine of climbing weekends in Wales and occasional road trips further afield was fun, reassuring and generally epic free.

The following year, in the summer of 1975, Tom, Leigh and I climbed the famous, 450-foot high, red sandstone sea stack known as The Old Man of Hoy in the Orkney islands, twenty miles off the northernmost tip of Scotland.

The iconic Old Man definitely measured up to all our expectations. A rare spell of warm and sunny weather saw Tom, Leigh and myself leaning on the deck railing of the St Ola car ferry and staring wide eyed as we passed by the banded, ochre colored monolith from across the turbulent, foam capped waves. All around us, tourists were avidly shooting photos. It suddenly struck me that merely setting eyes on the Old Man was the endgame for most people on this packed ferry, while we were here with a resolute purpose. The St Ola ferry was merely our method of conveyance.

Still, the panorama was cutting edge spectacular, with the Old Man's slender finger dwarfed by the heady backdrop of the magnificent 1100' high cliffs of St John's Head, a truly forbidding stretch of coastline, alive with the screeching and swirling of abundant bird life. We were about to embark on an adventure that no other tourist could ever dream of.

Suffice to say, it was an almost flawless excursion and a much-needed success that helped boost our self-confidence and renewed that nagging desire to explore and climb up high in faraway places.

It was only after the summit photos, followed by a mildly complex rappel descent and then the relief of safely reaching the ground, that a Fulmar Petrel Sea bird popped out of a rabbit hole and barfed reeking fish guts all over my leg.

Chapter 3. Coming to America

Steve Woosey, (aka the Wooze) was a gangling, bespectacled nerdy chemist who turned up one night at another one of our raucous Wednesday night club meets. He was dead set on mastering the art of rock climbing, so with a whopping four years of climbing know-how under my belt, I set about teaching him the basics.

Wooze was a total star. He drove a slightly dilapidated bright red Triumph Spitfire and was a highly inept motorist, who had twice failed to pass his driving test. The weekend trips to and from the Gwydyr hut and to the crag in his sports car became far more adventurous than the climbs we trained on. We became great friends, but that friendship soon became a little strained when Laura entered both of our lives.

She was a beautiful, lithe, vivacious, and dedicated ballerina with dark, flowing hair, deeply penetrating eyes, and a captivating smile. She had just started dating the Wooze when the whole Gwydyr gang descended upon a completely mental climbers' party. It was a night of out-of-control boozing and wild, manic dancing. In the midst of it all, Laura grabbed me, and we danced to the deafening crescendo of a Led Zeppelin song. Suddenly, she drew me towards her and gazed longingly into my eyes. Both completely unable to resist, we kissed with such an upwelling of raw intimacy. It was moments later when I realized that I'd just fallen completely in love with her.

In the coming months she dated me, and then dated my best friend, and then me all over again. The ensuing love triangle practically destroyed the both of us.

One particular evening was spent moping around Wooze's house. Neither of us saying a word. We knocked back beers followed by a whole bottle of gin, and I literally broke down and began sobbing tearfully into my glass. I felt so ashamed. How the hell could this one woman put such an emotional smack down on two once happy and contented souls as us?

The breaking point came weeks later with a huge gathering of climbers descending upon the sea cliff climbing areas around Bosigran in Cornwall for Christmas festivities. Some of the Gwydyr gang made a strong showing, Leigh McGinley, Tom Jones and many others, plus other climber groups from Bristol and Sheffield. I made the long 360-mile journey south with Laura and my younger sister Jan in my mum's old Triumph Herald and arrived at the remote, rural country pub in time for a hearty dinner. Leigh joined our table, and the evening was progressing nicely.

Then, incredulously, Wooze arrived completely out of the blue and sidled up to our table and my girlfriend. The evening ended up with Leigh and I completely passed out cold after just a mere eight pints of lager and Wooze absconding with the love of my life. She made her choice that night and I had to respect it. The double dating nightmare was finally over and even though we still remained friends, I returned home with a forlorn heart and a pressing need to leave my hometown of Wallasey to start a brand-new life, as far away from both of them as possible; at least for now.

The party town of Sheffield in South Yorkshire was the obvious choice. Squint lived there. He suggested that I come out and crash on his couch for a while, until I got my head straightened out.

He lived on Brunswick Street, a stone's throw from the university, which meant lots of dances, live music, and plenty of dateable girls. Bands like the Sex Pistols, Ramones, Stranglers, and the Clash had just landed on the music scene. Colliding with that kind of energy involved mosh pits and pogo dancing. Wild parties were the norm, that, coupled with the rediscovery of the rolling hills of the Peak District with it's long history of hardcore limestone and gritstone test pieces, completely eradicated any lingering memories of losing Laura.

As I settled into my new surroundings, a severe monetary issue soon began to rear it's ugly head. It slowly dawned on me just how giving my parents had been and how much I had taken them for granted. I had also relished telling my boss to shove that lousy printing job right up his rectum, so now I was flat broke. Various menial jobs and differing living situations eventually landed me in an epicenter of Jamaican culture, Harcourt Road; it was a vibrant place. Men with long, flowing dreadlocks, colorfully dressed in red, gold and greens. Loud rhythmic reggae music boomed from various doorways and always the fragrant waft of obscenely potent ganja and hashish.

I shared a house with four other climbers and so the focus was on getting stronger and braver whenever the weather was fine, but also getting revolving kneecaps drunk when it wasn't.

One day just before Christmas, we were invited over to have dinner across the street with five lovely student girls. It was a night to never forget, with delicious food, plenty of alcohol and endless stories around the dinner table. One of the girls was nicknamed Puddles, aka Pud.

She recounted the tale of when she was three years old, her uncle had her perched on his shoulders and he was bouncing her up and down. She was giggling so hard that she tinkled down his back, thus the name Puddles. We became close friends and quite soon started dating.

In the late seventies, jobs of any kind soon became a rarity. Margaret Thatcher was in power at the time and had pledged to do what it took to lower the current high rate of inflation. The unemployment rate soared to one in four in the inner cities. The daily hike down to the Job Center to find almost zero vacancies was soul destroying. Then one morning I applied for a position as a bus conductor and was accepted. I was issued a smart black uniform, a well-used leather money satchel and a ticket machine. Soon I was parading down both decks of a double decker bus and issuing tickets and collecting fares. Five weeks later I was transferred into driving school where I passed the tough Public Service Vehicle test and started driving buses. I had thwarted extreme poverty and was starting to make some decent money for once. Pud took notice of this pleasant change in my fortunes and having just finished with school, she decided to join me... as my bus conductress! We were a highly motivated couple, driven by our one common goal, to pay a visit to California's Yosemite National Park.

We worked together for a solid six months. Alternate weeks of morning and afternoon shifts were completely draining, with 4am starts one week, then 1pm starts the next. The bus garage canteen had a vending machine which offered up white bread sandwiches smeared in cold, greasy beef fat. Conversations with other crews usually revolved around how they got to annoy and/ or stiff their passengers.

There were fun times too. In an attempt to train for Yosemite, I completely ignored my bus timetable and raced through the center of town to the outer turnaround points, where I would attempt to do 20 chin ups (in sets of two!) on the bus shelter roof in the few minutes available. I went from a pathetic two pull ups to a whopping eight! Driving the last bus home after the pub closed was always entertaining. There would often be a passenger passed out cold upstairs, so I would have to stop the bus and try to shake him back into consciousness. If that failed then instead of calling the cops as per the rule book, I would leave him to experience a confused awakening, still on the bus, long after I'd parked it in the dark bus garage and gone home.

Social activities were nonexistent. We would either finish our shift after the pubs closed or be ready to just fall into bed exhausted in the mid to late afternoons.

We held on to our sanity and were finally ready to embark upon our great adventure. Joining us were Tom Jones and another Gwydyr climber, Dave Swarbrick. With trip anticipation at fever pitch we bussed down to London and that evening watched the recently released movie, 'Apocalypse Now' on the big movie screen. Our flight to Los Angeles was aboard the iconic and very affordable Freddie Laker skytrain. The drinks were complimentary. Excited beyond reason, we acted like four oversized alcoholic locusts and consumed multiple red wines, then four more bottles of wine, shots of whiskey and then finished out the flight with four more beers. UGH. Those were the days. Or were they? We made it through customs and immigration, then spent that Saturday night avoiding eye contact with scary looking characters in the LA Greyhound station, while dealing with severe jet lag and murderous hangovers.

Our bus eventually departed at 2am and we hit the freeways en route to Fresno and Merced. We gazed bleary eyed, as the first glimmer of rising sunlight cast rosy, salmon tinted hues across the vast forested landscape. After enjoying our very first American diner breakfast, we devised a plan to part ways and hitch hike as two pairs along the last 80 miles to Yosemite Valley. Pud and I made the trip in just three rides, with the final pickup truck driven by Phil Bard, a local climber and valley expert. He pulled over at a scenic viewpoint and allowed us our first glimpse of the immense monolithic profile of El Capitan. Over three thousand feet of dizzying rock features, dotted with teams of climbers that seemed lost in it's vastness and almost too small to be seen with the naked eye.

In the days following our arrival, we set about bagging as many classic valley rock routes as possible. Pud was strictly a non-climber and so spent her days sunbathing and reading down by the Merced River or exploring the many unique hiking trails around the valley. Phil turned out to be rock climbing's version of Yoda and bestowed priceless climbing route beta on the three of us. He took me under his wing and selflessly repeated a hit list of some of Yosemite's finest routes with me.

And so, despite many days of early season rain and snow showers, we became a little fitter and stronger, with our crack climbing techniques improving daily.

Then, on the 12th of May, Dave and I attempted the popular West face of Rixon's pinnacle, a 500-foot crack climbing gem. Dave led the second pitch, making bold moves through the size dependent crux moves.

Soon after, he reached easier ground and stopped placing protection. A very wrong move. He was thirty feet out from his last piece when he reached into the back of a small ledge and reefed on a block without testing it first. The block broke loose, and he pitched off backwards, hit a ledge ten feet below and took a seventy-foot upside-down fall, coming to a jolting stop level with me and fifty feet off to my right. Blood was oozing down the face below him, and he was unconscious and still upside down, so after screaming his name over and over to no avail, I began to attempt to lower him down the face back to the ground. Other climbers had heard the screams and had arrived at the base. Mercifully, he touched the ground with absolutely no rope left to spare. Panic stricken but with a feeling of huge relief, I rappelled to the ground in time to catch the distant siren of an approaching ambulance. He had regained consciousness by now but was probably suffering from a concussion. I fought to try and untie the knotted rope from his harness, eventually cutting it free with a knife. He was stretchered to the waiting ambulance, and we were driven at high speed with sirens blaring to Yosemite's medical center. Dave was wheeled inside while I sat on the bench outside, immersed in a state of worry and trembling internally, as I relived the horrific events of the day.

The doctors decided to keep him in overnight for observation. He had been extremely lucky; escaping with just four stitches on his forehead, widespread bruising to his head and body, a broken nose and lacerations to his legs and buttocks, presumably from him wearing thin, nylon shorts and me having to lower him down the rough, coarse-grained granite back to the ground. I returned to visit with him later in the evening with a pint of marble fudge ice cream. The stuff was so good that I consumed half before I arrived. What kind of friend was I? Really?

The next day, two other British climbing friends, John Kirk and Sid Siddiqui, climbed the route and retrieved all our climbing gear for us. Later that day Dave was released, and life soon returned to normal. I re-climbed the route with Tom two days later, finding Dave's pitch much harder than expected. We got rained on up near the top but struggled through and completed the route.

Yosemite continued to offer up more of her finest climbs to us. We dwelt in the notorious Camp Four campground, a dirtbag climber's haven, which meant loud, raucous get-togethers every night with a growing hotchpotch of kindred climbers from around the globe.

Two weeks later, I was sipping hot tea at our picnic table, savoring the aroma of damp forest after a night of steady rain, when a sudden, deafening clatter of rockfall reverberated through the forest. In a split second, death seemed imminent with the threat hidden from view by the tall, dense clusters of trees. Terrified, I looked around and suddenly realized that trees were shaking, and parked cars were bouncing around in unison, like well-choreographed disco dancers. After maybe ten or so seconds but what felt like forever, the quake subsided, leaving a stunned silence in camp, followed by intermittent whoops and screams of delight as the danger passed.

This had been a serious earthquake, a 6.5 on the Richter scale. It's epicenter was near the town of Mammoth Lakes, just

40 miles away. Believing it to be just one isolated tremor I continued with my plans to climb the South Face of Washington column, a popular 1200-foot big wall, situated across the valley from the spectacular profile of Half Dome.

After last minute preparations my Canadian partner Steve Labelle and I set off for the wall, arriving at a truck sized ledge after slogging up steep terrain with our oversized haul bags, stuffed full of climbing gear and enough food and water for our two-day ascent. Sad to say, the climb above was occupied with three other climbing teams, so we sat on our bags with backs to the wall and gazed in awe at the endless panorama of distant peaks. Out came the pipe and we smoked contentedly while considering our next moves.

Suddenly and without warning came the terrifying rumble of another giant tremor. 1200 feet of rock above us started to rattle and shake. A helmeted climber above took a fall onto his rope as I raced around the ledge in blind panic, reflexively seeking shelter from falling rocks but finding none and getting pelted with mere pea sized chunks of gravel. Astoundingly, nothing bigger came down, but as the quake subsided and frantic breathing returned to normal, another epic drama unfolded before us. Across the wide-open valley and to the right of Half Dome, an entire cliff, perhaps four hundred feet high suddenly peeled away, cutting a vast swath through the forest below and filling the entire valley in a cloud of dust. Without another thought we abandoned our haul bags and raced back to camp to relate our close call to friends. Apparently, similar epics had unfolded all over the park. Rumor had it that a tourist had died in the rockslide that we had witnessed. All trails were off limits and the road into Yosemite was also closed due to rockfall. Search and Rescue teams were stretched to the limit, rescuing teams of climbers off El Capitan and elsewhere.

I had recently met up with a highly focused, laugh a minute, hard climbing New Yorker by the name of Russ Clune. Russ recounted his tale of near disaster to us later that day. He had been working his way up the crux, open book corner pitch of The Good Book on the Folly when the earthquake hit.

Spring loaded protection devices known as 'Friends' had just been invented by Ray Jardine, who just happened to be visiting Yosemite at the time. As Russ straddled the corner and hung on for dear life, the 500-foot-high pillar twitched and all his protection fell out of the crack, that is, except for his 'Friends.' These sprung loaded camming devices, (also known as cams) absorbed the movement of the crack and potentially saved his life. It was amusing to watch a beaming Russ Clune stride across the parking lot and eagerly shake Ray's hand while thanking him for his invention!

With signs warning us of a possible 8.0 earthquake anytime, unease in the climbing community ran sky high. Four more aftershocks hit that night, but two days later on May 27th, Mount St Helens exploded in Washington State, releasing clouds of volcanic ash high into the atmosphere. It was declared the most violent eruption in US history causing an estimated 57 deaths and $1.1 billion in property damage.

A sign on the Camp Four notice board that evening read-
WARNING: 50% CHANCE OF A POSSIBLE 7.0 EARTHQUAKE

PLUS, A CHANCE OF VOLCANIC ASH FALLOUT FROM MOUNT ST HELENS

What a wild country. I was informed that a 7.0 on the Richter scale might be as much as 30 times more powerful than any previous quakes we'd seen so far. All trails stayed closed, and all trailheads were patrolled by the rangers. Despite this glitch, we still managed to bag the odd climb on what we tried to imagine were solid, 'quake free' cliffs. Looking down at the valley's exit road to El Portal from one such crag, we were astonished to witness a solid line of bumper-to-bumper traffic stampeding their way out of the park. We would soon have Yosemite Valley completely to ourselves, but the constant, nagging fear of facing cataclysmic earthquakes, deadly landslides and rockfall soon had us contemplating a hasty retreat.

Two days later, Pud and I jumped in with Phil Bard and beelined for San Francisco. Once again, Phil generously played the perfect tour guide and for two solid days waltzed us around some of San Fran's hot spots. Chinatown, Fisherman's wharf, Alcatraz, and Golden Gate Park to name just a few. It was a much-needed diversion from valley life, and we returned to Yosemite with renewed vigor, arriving back at our silent campsite at 1am. As I lay my head down on the pillow in my tent, I felt the low rumbling of one last tremor. The gods had said their goodbyes and had finally left us in peace.

I happened to spot the unmistakable mop of dark hair, pale blue eyes and charismatic smile of one Ed Webster in the campground the next morning. A world-renowned climber, Ed and I had first met back in Sheffield while he was giving a slide show on various sandstone towers that he'd climbed in the Utah desert. The show had been a much-needed break from my depressing, hum drum, bus driving lifestyle. I sat enthralled that evening, gazing at vivid images of his crazed solo first ascent of the 600-foot Primrose dihedrals on Moses' tower, to the tune of the Bob Dylan's hit song- Knocking on Heaven's door. That one inspirational slide show renewed my resolve to save enough cash to visit America and fulfill my dream.

Over the next few days, I tagged along with Ed and his girlfriend, Sue Patenaude and we picked off more Yosemite classics.

While sipping coffee at the lodge cafeteria one morning, Ed and I hatched plans to climb the 3500' long Salathe wall, on El Capitan. One of the most classic, multi day big walls in North America.

After spending a day racking gear and buying food, we sauntered up to the base, only to find two fixed ropes in place.

Dismayed at having to get in line below other climbers, we planned to return the following morning and fix our own ropes. After a leisurely 10 o'clock breakfast, we duly carried the haul bags to the base of the climb, curious to see how the other parties were faring, only to discover that the fixed lines had vanished and yet another team was now preparing to fix their own ropes. Clearly some shady tactics were called for.

"Hello, I'm Ed Webster. I've done an A5-5.11, 14-day new route this spring, plus the Pacific Ocean wall and The Nose route. Can we please go first if we don't fix ropes and just go for it?" They graciously agreed, but then we realized that we'd left our sleeping bags back in camp. Ed sprinted off to fetch them while I rattled climbing gear ever so slowly in a show of racking up, while awaiting his return.

We made it up just six pitches that afternoon and spent an uncomfortable first night partially hanging in slings. The rest of the climb went without a hitch, and we topped out three days later. It was a crowning moment in my life. In a state of awed wonder mixed with huge relief to be free of the clinging void, I gazed down upon the twinkling lights of the valley floor and all the feelings of joy and wellbeing peaked during that one, brief moment. There would have to be a lot more of this, I pondered to myself.

Chapter 4. The Grand Tour

"Even if you're on the right track, you'll get run over if you just sit there."
    ~Will Rogers~

It was now mid-June and blistering daytime temps were starting to get uncomfortable in Yosemite Valley, especially for pallid, white skinned Brits. In a spur of the moment decision, Pud and I hopped in the back of Russ Clune's Chevy truck and headed for Colorado along with Tom 'Stick Insect' Jones and Russ's climbing partner and college buddy, Gordon Banks. It was a one-way trip for Tom, Pud and I as we had no set plans and were dying to see more of this fascinating country.

We dropped Gordon off at his parent's palatial home in Aspen, Colorado and enjoyed a sumptuous breakfast with them while feeling a little scummy and underdressed. Russ was itching to reunite with his girlfriend, Melinda back in Boulder. She had rented a place for both of them, and Russ had arranged for the three of us to stay with another climber, Jim Gilcrest in a true Boulder climber's' hangout. It felt great to live under a roof again and in the coming weeks we prepared lavish meals with the group and hit all the bars on the bustling Pearl Street mall. My time in Yosemite had left me feeling stronger and fitter, plus living in a climber's household with a regular supply of partners meant coming to grips with Colorado classics almost every day.

In the space of just one month, we paid visits to- Eldorado Canyon, Estes Park, Boulder Canyon, The South Platte, Garden of the God's and even Vedauwoo up in Wyoming.

More bizarre weather phenomenon caught up with us one day when Russ and I got pelted by golfball sized hailstones high up on the fourth pitch of the Naked Edge in Eldorado Canyon. My pain induced screams were drowned out by the roar of the deluge as I witnessed a genuine flash flood and chaotic rockslides across the canyon. The storm was the worst in years but luckily it soon subsided. Severely shaken and frozen to the core, I surveyed my sleeveless arms and was shocked to discover that the hail bombardment had left angry, red welts all over my exposed skin.

Really? America never ceased to amaze me. Could there be any more geologic or weather weirdness left in this country's bag of tricks to taunt me?

One evening, while boozing it up in the Dark Horse pub, I spied some familiar faces from back home. Fellow Englanders, Roger Whitehead, Mick Lovatt and Duncan Sperry were finishing up with their visit to Boulder and were now planning to head out west to Tuolumne meadows in Yosemite's high country.

They had purchased a beater old Ford LTD station wagon. A very American looking machine that was almost nineteen feet long and weighed close to 5000 pounds! Even with gasoline at $1.19, this rig only managed about ten miles to the gallon and so they were very keen to pack the car with more passengers. They also shared our dislike for near 100-degree temperatures.

At 8600 feet, the glaciated, granite domes of the pristine Tuolumne wilderness were a much cooler option and seemed like the ideal solution to our woes. And so, the decision was made, and our group would hopefully leave in around two weeks' time.

After enduring eleven more, mainly pool bound, apathetic and sweltering days, our evening departure from Boulder was blessed with rose tinted rays of a beautiful sunset beyond the Flatirons. The non-stop, 24-hour drive reverberated with feverish talk of future ambitions, accompanied by the steady thrum of the big V8 engine, as we sped across the vast open rangelands of Utah and Nevada en route to higher, fresher and cooler climbing areas. During the trip, I recounted my recent ascent of El Capitan with Ed Webster. Roger suggested that I go for a double whammy and try to climb Yosemite's iconic landmark, Half Dome as well. It was at a higher elevation than El Cap which suddenly made it seem like the perfect goal.

Phil Bard was still dodging the heat in Yosemite when we arrived and when I broached the idea of the two of us attempting Half Dome together, he enthusiastically agreed, suggesting that we jump on the Direct Northwest face. This was an ambitious project, with many pitches of mixed aid and free climbing and requiring pitons as well as a large, varied sized rack of standard gear. After a long day of scrounging up equipment and making final preparations, we arose at 6am the following morning and sweated and grunted our way up the crowded tourist trail with two very overweight haul bags, arriving at the base of the wall at around 12.30pm. The 2200-foot face loomed above us, looking blanker and more foreboding than all the other walls that I'd seen. Nonetheless, we managed to climb four pitches that afternoon, then fixed ropes back to the ground for a very welcome final night on terra firma. We laid out our sleeping bags and settled in for some much-needed rest. I sauntered over to a nearby spring to fill up our gallon plastic jugs in preparation for three or four days on the wall. Crouching down by the trickle emanating from the base of the wall I was suddenly startled by the resounding 'whump,' of a football sized rock as it disappeared into the soggy, green moss right next to me. This single rock came out of nowhere and had probably been pitched off Half Dome's summit, 2,200 feet above by some ignorant tourist. It had free fallen the entire distance, hurtling silently and at warp speed. I imagined that my death would have been fairly painless had it not missed me by mere inches.

We awoke at sunrise to the twittering sounds of diving swallows and choked down granola bars before packing up and getting to work. Ascending the fixed ropes and hauling the bags up to our high point past a cavernous crescent chimney was taxing. Soon I was setting off into the unknown, feeling dehydrated and exhausted from the previous day's toil, but also acutely focused on the job at hand. Now fully absorbed, I used practically everything I carried on my rack to complete the pitch, even resorting to using a string of five skyhooks* in one spot. We continued to swap leads and haul the bags, steadily gaining height as a cooling breeze wafted across the face. The climbing was always mixed, with short sections of aid followed by free moves, which meant stepping out of stirrups and onto small teetering rock holds. No fun when toting a big rack of 'friends', pitons, a hammer, and other hardware.

Then at around 2pm, a scorching sun stole across the top of the face and without a speck of shade to cower in, we began to swelter. We were facing due west and so came the realization that this searing heat would stay with us, until a 9pm sunset finally relinquished it's grip on the glowing, cherry colored face. So much for Half Dome being cooler than down in the valley.

We climbed ten pitches that day but failed to make it to the Grand Terrace bivy ledge by just thirty minutes. With most of the difficult aid pitches climbed, the near total darkness forced us back down to the belay and a sleepless night spent half on the rock and half hanging in slings. Aching and stiff, getting an early start the next morning was a big relief. We would bag another eight, hard won pitches on this day, but halfway through the morning another volley of tourist driven rocks came raining down. These we heard coming. Terrified, we peered skywards, ready to fling ourselves out of the line of fire while screaming in unison at the top of our lungs for these idiots to stop dropping

* Small metal, sharp edged hooks which (hopefully) adhere to minute rock edges, allowing the climber to attach a stirrup and carefully step up and gain height.

rocks. We were about halfway up the face now and our screams may have actually been heard, for everything went quiet again, that is until half an hour later when a search and rescue helicopter came swooping in and hovered like an oversized hummingbird, safely out of any line of fire but dead level with us.

Someone had heard our screams and now presumed us to be in need of a rescue. Sickened and stressed out by all this unnecessary drama, we signaled to the chopper that we were ok, and she veered off to one side and sped away, leaving us to regain our wits and continue. Sun bleached and severely dehydrated; we finally made it to a fine bivy ledge known as Big Sandy by nightfall. We had joined up with the Half Dome's classic Regular route at this point and so the next morning's final six pitches contained more fixed hardware, allowing us to move faster, finally topping out by midday.

A small throng of tourists soon gathered and gazed at us with open-mouthed stares. Then Pud suddenly appeared out of the throng. We hugged and whooped and danced around, then hugged again. She had timed it perfectly and greeted Phil and I with a mouthwatering six pack of beer and carrot cake. Oh, how I loved this girl. We nailed the six pack in short order then had to scurry down the metal handrail descent in the face of a dark, brooding thunderstorm: the first in a week. We stumbled zombielike, down the nine miles of rain splattered trail in time for a lavish celebratory dinner at the Four Seasons restaurant.

It had been an incredibly successful climbing season for me, but now I was starting to sense the onset of a little burn out in my achievement goals. Tuolumne's magical granite domes and high mountain lakes lived up to their reputation for being cooler and more tranquil than the hustle and bustle of Yosemite Valley. Four days after our grand reunion on top of the Direct, Pud and I hitchhiked up to Tuolumne meadows and reunited with Phil and a group of other local climbers. This was just what we both needed. We took in a few peaceful backcountry hikes together, I also climbed a bunch of knobby, multi pitch dome routes when partners and motivation permitted, but it was very hard to pass up beer infused, group, nude sunbathing sessions down at the idyllic Tenaya lake beach. We spent many days there, in a state of complete contentment.

There was only one tiny glitch in our otherwise perfect existence. Cash. I'd already sold off a rope, a ratty pair of climbing shoes and a couple of cams to augment our limited finances.

While relaxing at the beach one day, Pud and I started to discuss the notion of doing the big hitchhike across the entire country to New York city, and then flying home. This theme became the focus of many future conversations. Then one morning after a hasty breakfast, we stuck out our thumbs next to the Tuolumne post office and decided to give it a try.

The following morning, we awoke in the open desert on the outskirts of Winnemucca, just off Interstate 80 in Nevada, where we unfurled our newly acquired road map. It both shocked and amused us to realize just how naive we'd been, having covered a mere inch on this very, very large map. The ensuing journey took us seven days, ten hours and a whopping fifty-six rides!

After only a short spell on the approach ramp, we were picked up and driven 450 miles to Salt Lake City by a rather shady looking character. Tim could have played a stunt double for Jack Kerouac. Right off the bat, he insisted that we pay him $13 for gas and buy him cigarettes, and a six pack of 16-ounce cans of beer. That night, very relieved to be free of him, Pud and I snook into a construction site and slept in a partially built house. It would be our last stab at sleep we'd have for quite a while.

After another lengthy 440-mile ride to a 'Little America' truck stop haven near Cheyenne, Wyoming, we became severely bogged down on the many ranch exits throughout Nebraska and Kansas and didn't sleep for almost three days. A mind-numbing life of either standing at the top of an interstate on ramp with our thumbs out and smiling at passing traffic, or spending the night hunkered down in a dreary truck stop diner, while awaiting the first glimmer of sunrise, so as to start the whole shitty gig all over again. One afternoon, the skies darkened dramatically, and a shrieking wind picked up as we motored through vast expanses of Nebraskan cornfields. Pud and I were very thankful to be safely inside the cab of another farm truck and not out in the open in the middle of nowhere. Especially so when a large funnel cloud suddenly dropped from the cloud ceiling at the far end of a nearby field. We pulled over and watched, completely mesmerized, with eyes glued to the tip, as the near tornado almost reached the ground before slowly rising back up into the clouds. In the space of just a few minutes we had just witnessed yet another event in nature's whacky bag of tricks.

Our journey continued with more short hops and little chance of grabbing more than a few moments of shuteye, then finally, eureka! A solid 600-mile ride to Detroit city in a big eighteen-wheeler with two hilarious, wise cracking drivers. We rolled into the warehouse district around dawn. One of the guys had suffered a bad back so I was offered $25 to help unload 400 crates of lettuce. Happy to oblige, and glad of the spending money I duly complied. Bad back guy went off to score some grams of Lebanese blond hashish and later, while we all stared vacantly at bugs on the windshield, a big Cadillac limo screeched to a stop alongside us and a tall, white-haired mafia 'Don' looking gentleman emerged, along with two, muscle bound, very thuggish bodyguards.

It was the boss of the trucking company. Our driver's faces turned white with shock as the henchmen tore open the truck doors and ordered them down and into the limo. It came to light that they had been joyriding around the country in this rig and were now in very serious trouble. Pud and I were too terror stricken to move, until boss man poked his head up into the cab and stated very matter-of-factly that if we valued our lives, we would vacate the truck immediately.

We grabbed our backpacks and sprinted off down the street, but only made it about fifty yards when a loud shout stopped us in our tracks. It was elderly, wheelchair bound man waving his cane in the air from across the street and beckoning us to come over and say hello. We must have stuck out like a couple of sore thumbs in this mainly black neighborhood for he barraged us with a slew of friendly, curious questions. "Where are you from? Are you enjoying your stay and, where are you heading to next?" Still in shock from the previous encounter, we breathlessly replied that we were trying to make it into Canada and up to Montreal via the Ambassador bridge."

"Oh, head down this next street here. Wait a minute. No. That one is too dangerous, you'll probably get mugged! Hike down the next street. Its a lot safer." We thanked him for his help and set off on a three-mile hike through what felt like a fairly scary downtown.

Those three miles were distinctly worrying. With Pud dressed only in a halter top and skimpy denim shorts and both of us sporting giant backpacks, we were the cutting edge of sore thumbs, so much so that ultimately, three different, well-wishing motorists honked their horns and pulled out of the stream of traffic to say hello and then offered exactly the same advice. If we don't get out of the city by nightfall, make sure we get ourselves safely into a hotel.

The level of relief that we felt when safely on our way north was overwhelming.

We continued up through Canada towards Montreal with a plan to drop down into New York State. This final leg of the journey and the memory of that very last ride of those fifty-six would stay with me forever.

Dog tired, we'd made it up to Montreal and were now wending our way wearily southwards. While sheltering beneath an overpass to avoid the cold, morning drizzle, a bizarre, Volkswagen Golf pickup truck stopped, and the driver offered us a ride.

Jake and Sandra were an elderly farming couple from Missouri. Really sweet folks, who offered to take us across the US border and into New York State.

We arrived at the border crossing fifteen miles later and were ordered out of the back of the truck by the border guard and escorted into the immigration building for questioning. Once seated in his office, the chief demanded to see our passports and started grilling us on our intended future plans. We informed him that we were just trying to make it to Kennedy airport in New York and then fly back to England. This reply seemed to appease him somewhat.

I went on to summarize our recent seven-day epic journey from Yosemite in detail. The officer looked up and raised an eyebrow as he paused, then abruptly announced.

"Welcome back to the United States. You guys be safe out there!"

After being detained for half an hour or so, our hearts warmed when we left the building and found our farmer friends still waiting patiently outside for us.

A little later, we mentioned that we were hoping to meet up with one of our friends from the climber household back in Boulder. Dave Marvin lived in Burlington, Vermont. He had insisted that we pay him a visit if we ever made it across the country.

Without so much as a second thought Jake and Sandra informed us that they would take us there... across Lake Champlain!

They detoured from their intended travel route and instead paid $15 for the car ferry, adamant as they were on getting us to our final destination. We were duly dropped off at a payphone in Burlington, but when I called the number, Dave's mother answered and informed me that he had just left for California that very morning.

Completely demoralized, Pud and I were far too weary to even think straight. All that way for nothing.

Jake and Sandra became even more concerned.

"Do you know anyone else out East," they ventured.

I thought for a moment.

"Well, I have a friend; Ed Webster, but he lives in North Conway, way up in the White mountains of New Hampshire."

A short pause, then,

"Hop back in. We'll take you there."

Astounded, we couldn't believe our good fortune. Meeting two of the nicest people alive, who drove us through Quebec, New York, Vermont and now New Hampshire, to our final goal.

At eight o'clock that night, as we hunkered down on Ed's doorstep, completely drained but inwardly beaming with utter relief that our ordeal was over, the garden gate opened and there stood Mr. Ed Webster and the lovely Susan Patenaude, both suddenly startled by the two scruffy intruders lurking in their doorway, amid our litter of empty, victory beer cans, their surprise turned to beaming smiles and big hugs.

In the coming week, we decompressed from our epic journey, and I teamed up once again with Ed and Sue for some pleasant scampering on the course white granite of Cathedral Ledge outside of town. One fateful evening I suffered an almost fatal mishap.

Ed and I were rappelling down from the top of the crag in the gathering twilight. Still seventy feet above the ground, I had rappelled almost to the very end of my rope and was intending to swing over to another ledge and another final anchor. Realizing that the arc of my swing would come up short of the ledge, I foolishly decided to clip into a protection bolt in front of me then free solo over to the nearby ledge.

Just as I was about to come off the rope and ease my body weight onto the bolt, it suddenly broke off in my hand. With only four inches of rope left beneath my rappel device, I had to frantically hand over hand my way back up the rope, with burning forearms, batman style, to rejoin Ed. It had been a really close call. We soon figured out a safer way down and made it back to the ground without further incident.

One week later, Pud and I resumed our journey and thumbed our way to the laid-back college town of New Paltz in New York State. It was now the beginning of September, and we were almost broke, more than a little homesick and very keen to get home. After a last foray at the Shawangunks climbing area above New Paltz, we caught a ride to Kennedy airport and purchased our standby tickets back to London with almost the very last of our cash. It must have been a busy weekend, for it took a crushing thirty-one hours before our names were called and our flight to Great Britain confirmed.

After the initial thrill of reuniting with friends and family again, getting back to my old, routine life became unbearably dull and anticlimactic. America had shown me things I hadn't believed existed outside of books and on television.

In the space of six months, I had witnessed earthquakes, mudslides, flash floods, golf ball-sized hailstones and funnel clouds. I had climbed El Capitan and Half Dome and had hitch hiked the breadth of the North American continent. I had fallen in love with that country and all the great friendships I had made there. It was the only place that I truly wanted to call my home. I just had to think of a way to make my dream come true.

Pud had different plans altogether. Our trip had been a bit of an 'ordeal by climbing' for the poor girl and although we had shared an unforgettable adventure together, she was now focused on furthering her education in Plymouth, Cornwall. We both cried when I hugged her goodbye at the bus station before heading off on my second, and much crazier American climbing trip, a year and a half later, in the spring of 1982. The four months that we spent apart changed us irrevocably and despite passionate letters and the occasional phone call, sadly, we broke up shortly after I returned home.

Chapter 5. Planes, Trains, and Automobiles

"Some people want it to happen, some wish it would happen, others make it happen."
~Michael Jordan~

It would be another four years before I married my sweetheart, Michelle and applied for permanent legal residency in the United States.

My boss had insisted that I get legal and start paying taxes immediately. My immigration attorney suggested that marriage would be one possibility and so I shamelessly proposed to six different women in about as many months. Their responses were both varied and oftentimes amusing, ranging from. "What would my parents say?" to, "Please buy me lots and lots of cocaine!" It was a total disaster; I knew this was completely wrong, but I kept extending the offer, nonetheless.

One close friend at that time accepted my marriage proposal in a very matter of fact way, as a favor to a friend, but when faced with the reality of dealing with a potentially fake marriage, it was I who immediately jettisoned the whole dubious scheme.

Michelle was the real deal though. She was a wildly spirited girl, having recently played lead singer in a hard rock band based out of Flint, Michigan. Michelle had just relocated to Boulder and a more settled existence and would soon attend Colorado University for her master's degree.

And she rock climbed too!

We decided on a church wedding in my hometown of Wallasey, near Liverpool and so I tasked Michelle with taking care of the travel plans. With wedding expenses looming, she went out of her way to track down the cheapest air fare and found one to Luxembourg. Unsure of exactly where that was, we peered intently at the revolving globe in our apartment and decided that Luxembourg was close enough to Britain to make the trip feasible. It was epic. First, we DROVE from Boulder to New York via North Carolina and Chesapeake Bay where we visited with friends and family. After staying with Russ Clune's family in Mamaroneck, New York and having a few drinks there, we dumped the car in Kennedy airport's long-term parking and FLEW to Luxembourg. Next, we had to take a TRAIN across the whole of Belgium to the English Channel and then catch a BOAT across that. Finally, we had to endure a 400-mile HITCH HIKE to my parent's house where we collapsed with utter exhaustion.

The wedding took place in the quaint old St Nicolas parish church down the street and was just beautiful. Lots of friends attended. Leigh, Stick Insect, Squint, The Yob, Zoe, Helen and Quentin to name just a few. We were festooned with wedding gifts, including lots of kitchen ware. We would never make it back to Luxembourg so heavily laden and had to change our flight at great expense and reroute through Reykjavik, Iceland, where we spent a bone chilling 24 hours sipping on some unpleasant local schnapps in a deserted lounge while awaiting our connection. To cap it all, having made it back to Kennedy airport, we spent an uneasy hour driving around long-term parking with the security personnel trying to locate our car. The 1800-mile drive back to Boulder along Interstate 80 was a welcome break after all that had happened previously.

Soon it was time to apply for permanent residency to the United States. The first of several immigration interviews did not go at all well, mainly due to my forgetting to mention on my application an incident that had occurred in Yosemite during my second visit there, four years earlier.

The Emergence of Bad Boy- (a very hazy recollection).

I really hadn't meant to offend anyone when I ripped off all my clothes and danced naked on top of the bar in Yosemite village. Although the tab that I'd chewed had given rise to some serious mischief, it was truly the Gallo white wine and gold tequila that made bad boy want to come out and play. Bad boy rarely came out, even when chemically summoned, but he was here now, fiendishly oblivious to reason and hell bent on brandishing MY frank and beans at a raucous, packed bar.

Among my many drinking partners in crime that night were Leigh McGinley and Steve Monks. They had only recently regained their wits, having been dead asleep all afternoon in their tents over in Camp Four. They'd had an excellent reason for such feats of lassitude; having just bagged the first British, one day ascent of El Capitan; in a sixteen-hour battle with The Nose route.

After a brisk night on top without sleeping gear, my friends had bashed down the East Ledges descent route around dawn. We had reunited at the pull-out by the Merced River and rejoiced, praised, and then toasted their ascent with ice cold breakfast beers.

They drank like kings but sagged to their knees after only a few hours: Exhaustion quickly overcame them, and they turned in for some urgent rest; leaving me to go it alone.

And go it I did, for not only was I still thirsty, but I'd already heard rumors of a 'happening' swimming hole high up in the rocks above the Ahwahnee Hotel. I deemed it my holy mission to go and see for myself.

After a short bus ride and an energetic scramble, I was greeted by an unlikely posse of well-tanned naked girls; hovering in close proximity to one equally naked 'famous guy.'

This was no ordinary naked 'famous guy.' This was Warren Harding; a multigenerational valley guru, a man revered for his bold, pioneering ascents and a knack for standing tall in the face of potentially lethal amounts of white wine. The day quickly transmuted into one, twisted glugathon and I smiled inwardly at this day's uncanny turn of events. Here I was celebrating my best friends' one day ascent of El Cap with the guy who made the very first ascent almost twenty-five years earlier!

By noon, the party was already 'way out of hand' and getting much more so. Later, we adjourned to the bar in Curry Village and sixteen hours after those first victory beers, my alcohol abuse had wreaked havoc to a point where forward bodily movement could only be made with the assistance of solid, inanimate objects. The midnight retreat from the Curry bar back to the Lodge bar was a grotesque, gyroscopic ordeal, similar to stumbling around a ship's deck in a severe hurricane. Luckily however, this bar was far too packed with people to fall down in, and so I launched myself off the doorway towards the back table and slumped in beside other spitting, shouting drunkards. Absolute heaven.

"Whuzzurpph?" I slurred. Upturned pitchers and pools of beer covered the table, and all eyes were thick with a shining, boozed-up glaze.

A heated but rambling discussion was in progress. Although animated, its content was drab and nonspecific. The evil that lurked within me hankered for much more peculiar antics.

"Hey Leigh. Let's liven up this dump…Pay half my fine…. OK?"

The Mountain Bar was just heaving with people and required absolutely no livening up, but I still saw fit to strip down just in case. Moments later, I'm running along the top of the bar above a heaving, demented crowd.

Amid all this frenzied dashing about, I suddenly powered straight into an overhead ceiling beam. Thwack! This was definitely not in the brochure, for now I was suddenly laid out naked on the bar.

The crowd went mental, and a minor riot broke out. Buckets of ice were tossed in my direction and precluded any chance of passing out cold. I wobbled back to the table and redressed, only to be informed that 'they' had called the rangers and that 'I' must vacate the bar or be arrested. Sadly, my legs could no longer be willed or suckered into cooperating. Standing upright was certainly not an option, so I was forced to sit in the corner and clutch my bruised noggin while sadly awaiting my fate.

Sure enough, although I could probably have escaped by crawling away on my belly using mere elbow propulsion, the rangers finally did arrive and twenty minutes later I was plucked out of the bar and summarily jailed.

The first thing I noticed when I lifted the blanket off my face the next morning was jail scenery; the wire mesh walls, the evil shitter, the locked cell door. At first, I was a bit puzzled, and it took a moment before I could recall exactly what bad boy had done to land me in such a terrible predicament. Then it clicked. Oh no…Oh no, not that!!! Surely, I didn't do what I just think I did! Curling into a fetal position, I began gnashing my teeth with chronic embarrassment.

Raoul Kantu was a real fruitcake. The stocky Mexican drifter had been brought in during the night for illegal camping and had kept everyone's attention by screaming for Thorazine.

"What a total nutbar," I'd thought; before passing into a deep, pre-dawn coma.

That morning, my predicament took a huge turn for the worse when I found myself handcuffed to the demented psycho and frog-marched barefoot across the village square; past the cemetery and into the courtroom, for a disheartening ritual known as arraignment.

Budummn-hh… budummn-hh! The hangover had focused all its energy on separating my inner skull from the pickled brains inside, resulting in searing spasms of pain.

Just me and Raoul handcuffed together, waiting for the judge. The jailer guarding the door and throwing us the odd disdainful look. Suddenly, Raoul started foaming at the mouth and growling to himself. In a flash, he slammed me in the side of the face with his fist, and we went bouncing down the steps and into middle of the courtroom; locked in a life-or-death battle, with fists flying in all directions. The jailer jumped in and broke us up as Judge Pitts strolled nonchalantly past and giving us both the evil eye.

"What the hell kind of weird legal system is this?" I thought to myself.

We were speedily dealt with and thrown back in the slammer.

The meeting with the judge hadn't exactly gone to my liking. Not knowing about due process or arraignment, I'd hoped to pay a small fine then go off and brag about my night in jail. But with an unwelcome charge of indecent exposure hanging over my head, my bail price was incredibly high. I would have to stew in jail until the next court hearings in five days' time.

Boo bloody hoo.

Judge Pitts seemed to be having trouble maintaining his composure and keeping a straight face during my appearance on the stand.

Through cross-examination, it was revealed that I had already spent two months grubbing around Camp Four, when the maximum legal stay limit was only two weeks.

I pleaded with the judge to give me just enough time to climb one more wall, but when he cast an eye toward the prosecuting attorney, the man just looked up and shook his head.

The judge's dramatic conclusion has stayed with me to this day and might be worthy of an Oscar. Proof that some form of primitive humor might actually exist in an otherwise callous, deadpan legal system.

"Well Mr. Hughes. You've climbed the walls. You've climbed the bar. You've climbed the tables and chairs…. Now I think it's time that you left."

For all my disorderly conduct and errant behavior, I was banned from Yosemite National Park for one long year. Nothing else, just that.

The punishment appeared overly harsh to me until a week later, when Leigh and Steve narrowly survived an epic storm and a harrowing retreat from high on El Cap's Pacific Ocean wall.

Having been legally ordered to miss this terrifying ordeal, I felt sufficiently moved to send the judge a quick thank you note.

I very much doubt that he received it though.

(Footnote-)

A differing account of this episode has since resurfaced, suggesting that there may have been two separate nude events. Mercifully, I can only recall there being one.

The aftermath.

The immigration officer was highly irritated. I bitterly regretted that high spirited act of complete stupidity, which I had hoped would never resurface again.

And now here it was, about to ruin my life all over again.

My application for permanent residency was put on hold pending a thorough examination of all the details of this extremely embarrassing incident. Mercifully, it only took a brief letter from the park service to clear it up. I was issued a conditional green card and began to build a more settled life in Boulder, Colorado. A year later Michelle and I were called into Denver's immigration office to prove that our marriage was still legitimate.

Our INS examiner was a thoroughly efficient and shrewd Scandinavian looking lady that could probably sniff out bullshit from many miles away. After a brief introduction and some intense staring from behind her enormous desk, the questioning began in earnest. "Could we show her our joint tax returns?" "ERM NO." "What about children's birth certificates. Did we have any kids?" "ERM NO" "Do you have ANY proof at all that your marriage is real?" "ERM." This interview was not going at all well. We were a committed and loving couple but had little proof of authentic wedlock except for our family album, which consisted mainly of wedding and climbing pics and lots of photos of our dog named Wuffies.

Wuffies was our adorable Husky/German Shepard mix who had been with us since he was six weeks old. He was our baby, and we did everything together.

Then suddenly it hit me. This lady might also be an avid dog lover!

Scattered around her desk and on the wall behind her were framed pictures of a very cute looking German Shepard. After poring through our album intently, her face suddenly lit up and her frosty demeanor vanished. We shook hands as she informed me that we had proven ourselves to be a happily married couple and that I would be granted permanent resident status. Wuffies had saved me! The dream had come true and the place that I truly wanted to call home was now officially, my home.

Chapter 6. Wall Season

"It isn't the mountains ahead to climb that wear you out; it's the pebble in your shoe."
~Muhammad Ali~

As Michelle, Wuffies and I settled in to a secure and contented new chapter of our lives in Boulder, Colorado, climbing trips near and far soon became the norm.

It was around this time that I developed a fondness for making first ascents. Michelle was full of encouragement for my obsession, and we spent many happily focused days hiking in to remote, back of beyond crags in Lost Creek Wilderness and the South Platte. Another granite crack preserve in the high prairie country of Southern Wyoming, known as Vedauwoo was another favorite of ours. Unfortunately, Wuffies liked to chase cows on occasion, which could mean trouble, but he would usually come running back to me if I yelled out the words.

"Oh-Yoo-Hoo, Wuffies!!"

This almost caused me to receive a beating when I shouted the same call from across main street in Laramie to our dog, who perked up in the back of my Chevy pickup truck when he heard his name called. A couple of cowboys perked up too, but luckily our dog's charisma and waggy tailed charm managed to win them over and avert bloodshed.

Besides Michelle, another favorite climbing partner of choice back then was fellow Englishman; Steve 'Crusher' Bartlett, who I'd first met back in 1983. It was purely a chance meeting, as the pair of us hovered vulture-like, around a free food buffet at Boulder's Broker inn, during a brief spell of mutual poverty. We became the best of friends and shared some epic adventures together; most notably, the fifth ascent of the notorious Hallucinogen wall in Colorado's Black Canyon of the Gunnison. Accompanying us was my triple jumping, hardcore climbing accomplice from the Gwydyr Mountain Club, Leigh McGinley.

This impressive 1800-foot big wall was first climbed back in 1980 by a team of four old school bad asses; one of which was my previous partner back on El Capitan's, Salathe Wall; Ed Webster.

Their first ascent was an outstanding achievement for its time and included a level of bold and impressive aid climbing only previously enacted upon the blankest sweeps of El Cap granite, high above Yosemite Valley.

Once we'd set our sights on this somewhat ambitious prize, the wheels of gear borrowing were set in motion. Multiple ropes and a giant rack of climbing hardware formed an impressive heap on the living room floor, but try as we might, two more vital portaledges* were just not forthcoming. Of course, I had mine. A cozy single one person fold out cot, complete with a weatherproof flysheet. Poor Leigh had no option but to make do with my extremely uncomfortable big wall hammock, while Crusher put his analytical brain to work and equipped an eighteen-dollar, K-Mart garden lawn chair with nylon webbing from each corner to a single tie in point above his head.

After a brief tree demo and some vague assurance that the lawn chair might actually work on vertical rock, my truck was loaded with two enormous haul bags, water jugs, ropes and then a third pack containing a tape deck the size of a small

---

* A lightweight, fold out cot designed for sleeping on vertical walls during multi day ascents.

suitcase, packs of Duracell 'D' batteries and about thirty taped music cassettes. If there was ever a prize for the most heavily equipped big wall team, we would surely win it.

After a scenic, 250-mile, high speed dash through the Central Colorado mountains we rattled down the final dirt road into the North Rim campsite, leapt out of the truck, hopped over the railing, and peered down into the shadowy depths of the Black Canyon below. Startled by the faint but unmistakable roar of the Gunnison River 1800 feet below, we began to sense the presence of the Hallucinogen Wall directly beneath us, but the sun had long since turned in and so we were left to spend the night writhing with fitful, uneasy dreams, fueled with the promise of the epic adventure to come.

The following morning, we strapped on our harnesses, replete with hula skirts of climbing gear then hoisted the colossal haul bags and set off down the steep approach gully to gain the bottom of the canyon. As the roar of the river grew louder, the faint breeze died away and soon we were pouring sweat as we took extreme care not to stumble and go crashing helplessly, like out-of-control turtles, down the steepening rocky steps garnished with shiny green clumps of poison ivy.

Finally, we arrived at a tiny beach alongside the river and doused ourselves with icy river water. The immensely forbidding wall before us rose up to a distant summit rim beneath a cloudless sky as we studied our rough topo drawing to try and identify various features that we would encounter. After filling the water jugs, adding iodine tablets and duct taping the lids closed it was time to rope up and start climbing. Luckily, the initial low angle pitches were moderate and so I quickly gained height and landed on a small ledge about two hundred feet up, then fixed our lead rope and descended back to the ground for our one last restful night on open, flat ground. As dusk settled in and dark shadows began creeping up the jagged, grey walls, the true magic of the Black Canyon came alive. Smoky shafts of amber sunlight threw every feature into sharp definition on faces over two thousand feet high. The thundering roar of the nearby Gunnison River became a soothing lullaby as we drifted off into a tired and undisturbed sleep.

Eager to commit to the wall, we began the gut-wrenching chore of hauling the bags up to our high point the following morning.

I jumared* the rope back up to the high point, tied back in, pulled up all the slack rope from the bags, ran that haul line through a lightweight pulley attached to the anchors, then clipped myself into the haul line on the other side of the pulley, my body weight thus acting as a counterweight to the bags below. I would still be tied into the anchors for safety, but with ten or so feet of slack rope. As the bags moved up a few feet, I would drop down a few feet, then jumar back up to the anchor and repeat the process again and again, until the bags eventually arrived at the high point.

But these bags were not going anywhere. Their immense weight, coupled with additional friction from the low angled slabs meant that brand new tactics would have to be called for.

I tied my extra tagline rope to the haul line and tossed it back down to my friends on the ground. Crusher (a tad heavier than Leigh), with his folded-up lawn chair clipped to his harness, clipped his jumars onto the rope and added his body as a counterweight as well as mine. It worked! The bags began their slow, upward journey, but as they moved up, Crusher would drop back down. He would end up jumaring 400 feet of rope before the bags arrived at the 200-foot-high point! We named our new system the 'Road to Nowhere' method, but at least we had a system.

---

* A handheld device that slides up the rope but locks in place when weight is applied, thus allowing the rope to be climbed.

As pitch followed pitch, the wall reared up and became steeper, making for much easier hauling. Later that evening, as we settled in for our first night on the wall, it became apparent that Leigh's crushingly painful hammock would allow for little or no sleep. After a solid thrash to gain entry into his sleeping bag, he would strike a sleeping pose, with his spine heavily curved and shoulders badly crunched together. Crusher however, seemed quite at home on his impromptu lawn chair as it dangled in defiance of gravity, above the abyss.

I awoke at dawn to the sound of swearing and thrashing emanating from the hanging olive green sack that contained a thoroughly pissed off Leigh. Next to him, Crusher reached over the top of his head, grabbed the aluminum frame and with a click, click, click, turned the top of his level lawn chair into a seat back. "Breakfast Mode," he announced, as he began scarfing a can of peaches and some granola bars. Soon, we were packed up and on the move. The climb gradually became more technically demanding. Being such an early ascent, the line to follow wasn't always obvious and involved some careful route finding and the occasional pendulum traverse to ensure that we stayed on route. We each took turns leading, or following to remove the gear, or counterbalance hauling. Both of my compadres climbed well and led hard sections of aid, resorting to hooking whenever the need arose and always to the sound of some of the more twisted and deranged music that the eighties had to offer.

We slowly gained height and settled into a regular routine of setting up our separate hanging cliff dwellings before dark. The weather remained perfect throughout. Two thirds of the way up I got dealt one of the hardest pitches on the route, seventy feet of nothing but hooks and graced with just three protection bolts. There is a definite artistry in this method of ascent. Making headway solely by caressing the wall to find a workable edge, selecting the most suitably shaped tip in your hook selection, placing the hook to see if it might hold your weight, then gradually transferring body weight by stepping up into an aider. * If it holds then step up all the way and clip into the hook, lean back gently and try to relax. The previous hook that supported your weight will usually fall off and dangle at your feet. Yes. Hooking requires a lot of finesse and a huge will to succeed.

For me, the most harrowing moment was right below the belay at the top of the pitch. Ten feet above my head was a fine, foot wide ledge and a solid, bolted anchor above it. My last protection bolt was twenty feet below and right in front of my face were a series of tiny, round holes that would require hooks with pointed tips, (known as bat hooks).

I was without these vital pieces and so had to place square edged hooks on the rim of these 1/4" holes. By some miracle my plan worked, and I arrived at the anchor sweating bullets, with my elated shrieks echoing around the canyon walls.

Although too narrow to sleep on, this incredibly exposed, foot wide ledge would serve as an ideal spot to hang our respective beds for the night.

The following morning ushered up the usual grunts and groans from the hammock, but this time accompanied with a whole lot more thrashing than usual.

"Oh God guys, I've got to 'make a poo'... Quickly!!!"

Crusher and I looked on in amused horror as poor Leigh eventually jumared out of the depths of his hammock up to the ledge, secured himself with a sling around his armpits, loosened his harness, dropped trou, leaned out... but... while a good portion of said poo cannoned down the hooks pitch below, plenty more landed on the ledge next to us, causing all of us to gag, retch and almost vomit. Then we realized that it was Leigh's turn to lead the next pitch and so, with a grinning apology, off he

---

* A short nylon ladder used to ascend on gear in aid climbing.

sped, leaving the two of us to frown and suffer in silence. But then Crusher, as always, came up with a plan. He dug around one of the haul bags and produced a small plastic tub of scented baby wipes. We rolled them up into straw shapes and shoved one up each nostril. Now we both looked like a couple of demented walruses, but at least the problem was solved without adding any vomit to the foul mix.

We were aiming for a prominent, beak shaped roof high up on the route. As the shadows lengthened, Crusher was busily aiding a finger sized crack leading up to the anchors beneath this enormous ceiling. We were dog tired and looking forward to settling in for another night; our fifth on the wall. Suddenly, Crusher let out a reflexive loud gasp as the medium sized, wired nut that he was hanging on suddenly dropped a short way down the crack and relodged itself again. With a slow, dawning horror he came to realize that the right side of the crack was actually a huge, twelve-foot-high flake that was now completely detached and on the brink of pitching into the void. Fighting to maintain composure and hardly daring to breathe, Crusher delicately intertwined a series of wired nuts, forming a floppy, two foot long 'cheater stick.' On the end, he added an aider, with the carabiner taped open with sports tape. Ever so gingerly, he reached at full stretch and just managed to hook the web of slings at the anchor. He scurried up the aider and was soon safely beyond reach of the death flake.

It had been quite a close call. Had that flake come off and the nut popped, it might have easily chopped Crusher's lead rope, sending him down with it.

There was very little light banter that evening, but with the arrival of a cheerful morning sun came a renewed outlook and a strong desire to reach the top that day. I led across the tippy top of the death flake, turned the roof on its right side and worked my way up the ever-steepening wall above. It was a thoroughly absorbing pitch and quite soon I was clipped into the next anchor and gazing in wonder at some incredibly complex and spectacular canyon scenery. Leigh cleaned the pitch and joined me with equally high spirits. As I scanned the other side of the canyon intently, I suddenly noticed a large gathering of people at a scenic lookout on the south rim, who seemed to be watching our every move. Some had cameras and others had binoculars trained upon us. I counted back the days since our departure and realized that today was probably a Sunday.

Crusher was about to give them the show of a lifetime. He was faced with having to cut loose from the anchor and pendulum fifty feet out into space. And this he did, but not before committing the enormous flake to the depths. The rock exploded with a deafening crash and filled the canyon below with a cloud of dust. Then out he sailed into space, with his trusty lawn chair strapped to his side.

Leigh made short work of the next, looser, and more broken pitch and after hearing the distant call from him, "Jumar when ready," I set off up the rope to clean the pitch and join him. I arrived at a large flat terrace and there he was, anchored into the back wall and with a slightly glazed expression on his face and... a beer in his hand! Four more lay on the grass next to him and to my amazement, they were still cold! Crusher joined us and the celebrations began. Then came shouts from the canyon rim not far above us. It was our friends, Olaf Mitchell, and Phil Broscovak. They had been enjoying a rest day from their own climbing endeavors and spent it watching us and knowing that we would make it out that day. They somehow wrangled a stuff sac with six beers on the end of a rope all the way down to us. We toasted to our ascent of this beautiful wall and then clinked cans one more time. "To the most beautiful canyon in the world."

"To the Black!"

Soon we were greeting Olaf and Phil on top with bear hugs and big grins. After six days of mainly hanging in a harness, the mere act of walking on flat ground, and even trying to change gear in my old truck was amusing and a little bit thought provoking at best. Maybe it was the beer too, but we didn't get very far that afternoon. Much as I was itching to get back to see Michelle, prudence dictated that we book into a cheap, roadside motel and proceed to drink a few more and then pass out cold.

Back in Boulder the next day, we were busily unraveling the morass of climbing gear on the same living room floor when the phone rang. It was my good friend Chip Wilson.

Chip was a highly enthusiastic partner who shared my passion for putting up new routes. He was also an avid desert tower climber and only lived about thirty minutes away from me in Golden. Chip was eager to hear all about our trip up the Hallucinogen, but then, out of the blue, suggested that Michelle and I accompany him out to Yosemite Valley where I might show him the ropes, literally, and take him up his first ever multi day big wall on El Capitan. I was still feeling 'battle hardened' from our recent adventures in the Black and was happily 'between jobs,' while Michelle was on Spring break. She assured me that she had plenty of studying to do during our absences, so long as we could climb together afterwards.

And so, even before my battered hands barely had time to heal themselves, Chip and I were roping up beneath the 1000-foot-high Leaning Tower, a short stroll across the meadow from El Capitan. This moderate route was first climbed in 1962 by Warren Harding along with various partners. The wall overhangs anywhere from 110 to 95 degrees, with long ladders of drilled (and very rusty!) rivets snaking through the blanker sections. It was deemed to be the perfect first wall for Chip to cut his teeth on and so it turned out to be. Two comfortable rock ledge bivouacs and three days later, we were back in El Cap meadows and speculating on what to climb next.

Michelle had a bit of a hissy fit when she heard we were going to get on Mescalito the day after next, and with good reason. One of the longest and most spectacular routes on El

Cap, this sustained mega classic weaves it's way through flawless expanses of golden granite for 2700 feet and 26 wild pitches. Retreat was reputed to be near impossible due to its steepness and the traversing nature of many of its pitches, especially after the notorious Seagull roof, a long line of ceilings six hundred feet up with a cavernous overhanging amphitheater below.

We planned for enough food and water for around seven days. Luckily, Mescalito sits on the southeast side of El Cap, so when the sun slinks behind the central buttress of the Nose route at around noon, cool updrafts of afternoon breezes kick in, so little or no thirst problems for us at all.

We began climbing and fixing ropes on the initial four pitches of the route as per the norm. Fixing alongside us on an adjacent route called 'Hockey Night in Canada' was Kurt Smith, another climbing buddy who hailed from Boulder, Colorado. Although thin and technically demanding, we made good time and soon had our ropes fixed and haul bags secured up at the high point. Now it was time to grow a pair, focus on the job at hand and commit to the long, unretreatable road ahead. Michelle decided to hike up with us and bid us farewell the next day.

Before our big send off the following morning, she mentioned that she might try and hike in to meet us at the summit, along with her new best friend Gloria, another equally high-spirited lass from Puerto Rico. They would snag a backcountry permit and plan on camping overnight before meeting us on top.

"What should we do about bears," she asked, with a slightly worried tone of voice.

I suggested that they maintain a clean campsite, hang their food high up in a tree far away from the tent, then as an afterthought advised them to lay down a circle of pee all the way around the tent. I struggled to maintain a straight face as we kissed and said our goodbyes. Michelle walked away and picked out a perfect flat rock to sunbathe and snooze on, while Chip and

I commenced our jumaring slogathon back up the ropes to our high point.

"OK, Oh Mighty Mescalito. Prepare to be boarded," I chuckled inwardly, as I surveyed the vast sea of open granite above and to the side of us.

As I led off into uncharted territory towards the daunting, horizontal Seagull ceiling above, I suddenly caught sight of a fixed rope, running the entire length of the wing shaped roofs, and disappearing around the right-hand tip, to where I hoped was the belay. Somebody had either chickened out or been forced to retreat in a storm. Either way, the rope provided us with a quick way of skirting one of the trickier and more time-consuming pitches on the route.

Trusting that the rope was securely anchored and not chewed by rodents, Chip launched out sideways in a dramatic display of bravado, clipped on his jumars and soon disappeared out of sight. Next, I unhitched the extremely heavy haul bags and lowered them out into space, until they dangled directly beneath Chip, allowing him to counterweight body haul them up to join him at the belay. Finally, it was time for me to follow the bags sideways and so I began to lower myself off the belay anchors and committed to the nerve-wracking horizontal rappel into the void.

Everything went as planned except the weight of the daypack that I carried tended to try and flip me upside down, causing me to exert much more strain on my arms to stay upright. When I arrived at the anchor severely winded, we both agreed that this daypack should join the haul bags instead of being carried by the second guy. The bag was duly clipped into what looked like a solid loop of webbing on the side of the haul bags and all seemed well, but then we both watched in a split second of stunned horror as the backpack came loose and went hurtling towards the ground.

Six hundred feet below us, we could just make out the blue bikinied figure of Michelle on her large, flat rock, as well as Kurt, who was a few pitches up his route, and also his climbing buddies milling around at the base. We screamed at the very limit of our lungs for everyone to scatter. "Look out! Rock-k-k!"

Michelle was on it in a flash. She heard the distant screams and the roar of the approaching missile and literally dove out of the way, as the bag exploded only twenty feet away from where she had been sitting. She had bloodied her shin in her rush to escape but was otherwise unscathed. I almost fainted with relief when I saw her raise one arm and begin waving up at us to let us know that she was ok.

A simple, stupid mistake on the climb had almost caused the death of my wife, or one of my good friends.

Pale with shock and trembling, we tried to take stock of what might have been in the bag. All our warm clothes, the camera, our cigarettes, some snack food, and our route description, the crucial map of where exactly Mescalito goes, what kind of climbing to expect, where to belay and how hard. Without it we were royally screwed and now we had just crossed into the zone where the easiest way off was probably upwards for another twenty or so pitches.

At the limit of our yelling, we could just about communicate with Kurt, a long way down below us. With little choice but to act, we decided to gamble everything. Tying into the anchor with only a couple of slings each, we untied from the lead line and knotted all our ropes together. First the lead rope, then the haul line, then the tag line and then the rope that we had just salvaged from the seagull roof pitch. At the end of all this, we attached a large rack of heavy metal pitons as an anchor weight, then began lowering. The rope behaved itself at first, but as it descended hundreds of feet down the face below, an impish wind picked up and started pushing the end of the rope and the rack of pitons in a terrifying pendulum off towards the Nose route! Backwards and forwards; the loud jangling of the pitons echoed around the cliffs. In all likelihood they were almost certain to catch in a crack or a flake and then we would be rendered completely helpless, but our heroic Kurt just managed to snag the end of our rope as it passed by him, even while he was in the middle of his own epic struggle to lead his pitch. A true miracle had just occurred.

Everything that could be salvaged from the boulder field was stuffed back into the shredded backpack which was then hauled up to Kurt and clipped back onto our train of ropes. Overjoyed and relieved beyond measure, we hand hauled the pack back to us in a frenzy of burning biceps.

Although we had lost all the time gained by cheating our way across the seagull roof, nothing else mattered but to avoid any more serious mishaps and work our way carefully up the route. Peregrine Falcons were out in force in the days that followed, and we marveled at their high-speed aerobatics and the sound of their unmistakable banshee screams echoing all around us. With perfect weather and totally absorbing and highly sustained climbing, long hard days were rewarded with shimmering, golden beams of evening alpenglow, as we finally stretched out on our respective single portaledges for nights of deep, exhausted sleep.

Many days later, pitch seventeen landed us at the Bismark ledge, one of El Capitan's finest room sized rock ledges. It was a place to lounge on and let the tensions of the previous days melt away. It also happened to be Michelle's birthday that day and so as the mild afternoon breezes gave way to the quiet stillness of evening, we lit a candle in her honor. The only thing that never made it back in the backpack was the cigarette lighter. The candle used up our last match, causing us to chain smoke our entire pack of cigarettes. Bouts of coughing and hacking resounded well into the night.

We topped out a few days later, on what might have been the most beautiful climb of them all. Back in camp the next morning I hugged my wife with such a loving intensity and with a resolute promise to never be apart like that again. She laughed and then recounted her attempt to meet us on top of Mescalito. Apparently, they had taken 'most' of my advice about warding off marauding bears. They spent a beautiful night out in the wilderness but had somehow managed to lose their way and so had to turn around.

We spent the last week climbing, hiking, and enjoying life together, before returning to Colorado to resume our everyday lives. It had been a spectacular time for all of us.

I had managed to climb fifty-four big wall pitches in just five weeks, but more importantly; Chip had now become a seasoned big wall climber and we had both lived to tell the tale.

Black Canyon of The Gunnison

Crusher's High-Quality Porta-Ledge

Crusher approaching the Beak Roof

Chapter 7. The Nefarious Nineties

"There I lay staring upward, while the stars wheeled over... Faint to my ears came the gathered rumor of all lands: the springing and the dying, the song and the weeping, and the slow everlasting groan of overburdened stone".
~J. R. R. Tolkien~

Climbing life in the early nineties was characterized by ambitious forays into the barren, red landscape of the Utah desert, spearheaded by the ever-dependable Steve 'Crusher' Bartlett. He was to become one of the all-time desert tower gurus. His recently published book - Desert Rock, was considered by many to be the ultimate historical and photographic bible for desert tower climbing.

The Enigmatic Syringe

I first encountered the soft, claylike rock of Monument Basin during an early ascent of Standing Rock, not too long after my lucky break with the kindhearted immigration lady. It was a kind of celebratory, 'welcome back to the fold' event for me. Joining me on this trip were Leigh McGinley and Chip Wilson. We were relatively new to the soft, desert sandstone game back then and none of us were feeling gallant nor overly brave, as we each took turns to grapple with the various bands of 'moistened kitty litter' rock that held this enduring monolith in place.

During frequent lulls, I found ample time to loiter around the base and peer into a monster telephoto lens that I had recently inherited. Zooming in upon a surreal world of crumbling cracks and tantalizing summits, the camera intruded upon these complex surroundings and drew distant vistas over to my neighborhood.

Far across the basin floor, one column of mudrock caught my eye repeatedly. A meaty trunk that rose up then stopped abruptly, while a pencil thin needle of rock continued skywards from atop this. "Hey guys. Don't you see? I swear. It's a perfect, hypodermic syringe-shaped tower."

It could have been over a mile away from where we stood though. Too far away for absolute certainty. Indeed: that upper needle might have been nothing more than just a separate mini spire rising up from the talus slope behind the main trunk. Two towers or just one tall one. The agony of doubt persisted throughout the trip. I squinted long and hard through that lens, but all to no avail. We ultimately bagged the eighth ascent of Standing rock since it's first ascent, twenty-five years earlier.

But still we left without ever knowing the truth about the Enigmatic Syringe."
Monument Basin Overlook.

Twin creases formed like ski tracks athwart snowplow brows. Near a vast drop to the other desert floor below, a solitary figure stood brooding - quietly shaking with bitterness and in turned loathing. On the bed of the truck, a vital part of his precious cargo – twenty-three bottles of imported lager were smashed to pieces inside an ice chest awash with amber foam, beer labels and ragged shards of broken glass.

"My Preciousss-ss." I mirrored the contorted face of Bilbo Baggins as he spied the one ring on a chain around Frodo's neck. "That strong lager was all mine dammit… mine, I tell you. mine…!!"

Of course, blame lay not with the bone shaking, second gear safari along Canyonland's White Rim Trail. No. Blame fell squarely upon the motorist. Upon me to be exact.

My absentee climbing partner had kindly offered up his Toyota for desert sacrifice.

I thus became wildly thrilled at the prospect of returning to Monument Basin.

Sadly, I was too thrilled not to run out of gasoline in the middle of Castle Valley while en route. Moreover, I was also too thrilled not to buy canned beer instead of bottles.

Four long years had passed since first catching sight of what came to be known as the Enigmatic Syringe. An eternity plagued by never knowing if the tower was real, or merely a devilish trick of distance and light.

But I came back alone and stopped by the rim to watch a setting sun cast spells of blood across that jagged, forbidding world. In the gathering gloom, I cracked the one surviving beer, leaned over the edge, and peered into the shadowy depths of the basin. Not a trace of anything pointy. Too bad. This particular mystery would just have to wait until morning.

Night fell and with it came fitful uneasy dreams, enhanced by an absence of lager. Unsettling images of a pencil thin tower beneath a shimmering canopy of stars.

With great relief, I awoke at third light, reheated some old coffee and choked on a bagel.

Unable to contain my curiosity for one moment longer, I hoisted the tattered haul bag, and proceeded at a brisk pace along the white cap rock towards the alleged whereabouts of my tower. The morning had come alive. The seemingly barren landscape had seen fit to unfurl a flowery blanket of vibrant color, with cacti and sagebrush shimmering to the caress of a warm spring breeze.

Anticipation rose with every step.

All those years of waiting and now a possible first peek at some improbable untrodden summit.

Then it occurred to me. I was so thoroughly obsessed with this discovery; like an addict whose drug of choice just happened to be a syringe shaped spire. Surely the craving stemmed from a much deeper addiction: an irrepressible desire to explore our rock-strewn world and cast eager eyes upon its infinite climbing possibilities.

Drawing closer, I felt the stirrings of some bizarre unwelcome memory. Of what though? I strained all my powers of recall and dredged up a long-forgotten tale of great woe.

A long time ago, I made an ill-advised bet with Barry Hurley, a jovial, Eastender from old London town.

Next to our worksite, there existed one very ugly fence built entirely from upright, brightly colored skis. We pontificated loudly as to how many skis went into its construction. Finally, it was loudly decreed (suggested by Barry's unscrupulous and mischievous brother, Alfie), that whoever lost the bet would have to work the whole next day, while wearing women's lingerie. i.e., cupped bra, fishnets, and frilly panties, in addition to a tool belt.

That following morning began with serious, life-threatening hangovers. A breakfast chewed in silence, prior to the drive of shame to begin counting skis. Upon arrival however, we were both too nervous to even look at the fence. We miscounted. Tried to count those skis again but lost track. One more time but still we fumbled it.

Now, as I drew closer to a possible viewpoint for the Syringe, a similar dread feeling crept upon me. What if it did not exist? What if I had wasted all these years agonizing in vain? What if I had failed to guess the correct number of skis? Fishnets? Oh-please-no!!

Too nervous to peer in that direction, to peer over the edge. Fifty yards from the desert rim. Forty. Thirty. Cannot bear to look. Twenty.

And suddenly there she was. A magnificent freestanding tower, replete with a main trunk and what looked like an absurdly thin, ninety-foot finger of rock resting on top.

Thin enough to hug like a bear!

The ascent was harrowing at times but also involved some sporadic drilling on the pencil thin 'hypodermic' section. In my rush to leave town I had packed a hand drill but no bolts and made the top with no angle pitons to spare for an anchor. A sketchy down climb and a single point rappel from the highest fixed aid piton was terrifying at best, but once back on solid ground there came a rush of euphoria that no drug could imitate.

Somehow, I had climbed the tower alone and then lived to drive away in search of fresh supplies of lager. The desert exhaled, cactus blossoms faded, and a lonesome forlorn wind returned that few noticed.

In late autumn, I returned once again. Same Toyota. Same basin. Different brand of lager.

The truck's owner, Steve 'Crusher' Bartlett straddled the cab roof and scrutinized the basin with powerful binoculars like some desert storm tank commander. I was not straddling anything. The half dozen cans of domestic swill that I had forced down my gullet and occasionally spilt in my lap had altered my ability to drive, operate machinery or refrain from swaying.

We were gazing at perhaps the largest unclimbed spire in Monument Basin and a very enticing crack system that begged for our attention.

"Let's hike down there and wage war on that pile." I slurred lightly.

Half a minute passed in silence. "You know something Strappo, I think that tower might even go free!" remarked Crusher.

I slumped back into my folding chair and tried to ingest this latest piece of info.

We exist to wonder, seek, and be awestruck by our findings.

"Oh god, I groaned. Here we go again."

~ Dedicated to the memory of the deer that I hit in Crusher's borrowed truck and to a cross-dressing carpenter who still owes me a day of work.

Remote pointy thing

Author on the remote pointy thing

Chapter 8. Whimperings

"When people keep telling you that you can't do a thing, you kind of like to try it."
~Margaret Chase Smith~

The solemn vow that I'd made to myself in the French alps, after my second near catastrophe as an aspiring young alpinist was, in reality, never going to stand the test of time.

"To quit all this climbing crap for good," should have come with a disclaimer, for fate stepped in and I was suddenly and willingly, thrust back into the arena of scary, high mountain climbing again, this time in Pakistan.

And so, it had begun.

As I finally floundered into base camp, whimpering plaintively from beneath a towering haul bag, my eyes began to revolve in opposite directions to my kneecaps. I slowly keeled over backwards and collapsed; corpse-like, amid lush meadow grass, alive with honeybees and the fragrant scent of unknown flora.

Coincidentally, I had arrived at a similar state many months earlier while at a party, having downed at least twelve pints. It was well into the party and all kinds of verbal crap was spewing forth. Dave Towse was busy twittering on about a supremely beautiful Karakoram peak known as 'Ladyfinger,' a.k.a Biblimotin (6000 meters).

He had attempted the unclimbed southeastern wall five years earlier. It had been late in the season and cold days with unrelenting snow and bad weather had forced him to abandon ship.

"Bla, bla…," he droned. "No peak fee or irritating Liaison Officer required…Only five hours to base camp from town… even have a portaledge and pins stashed up there."

I pondered. It really did sound like an excellent venture. The poor guy was obviously dying to give it another go, but what the hell was the catch?

Dave paused for a moment. "There's only one minor snag though," he said. (Ah-hah!)

"Erm…Rockfall on the approach tends to be a little bit on the dangerous side."

Many seconds passed as my barely functioning brain cells failed to register this quite important data.

"It'll be an absolute and total p-path," I slurred, as my eyeballs dissolved into a sea of lager.

A few hectic months later and we were finally ready to face the vast and mighty Karakoram peaks. All my brave talk had long since turned into pantywaist.

Our team consisted of Ladyfinger veteran; Dave Towse (Brit) and seasoned alpinists Gavin Jordan (Brit) and James Donnell (Georgia boy). Together with fourteen heavily laden but tireless porters, we swanned into base camp and assumed similar chest-heaving and jelly-like positions. As the heavy breathing subsided, we gazed in awe and disbelief at the surrounding peaks. All seemed closely guarded by enormous serac* walls and bleak avalanche-raked couloirs.

I peered up the valley and my heart skipped a beat. Lady-finger had suddenly shed her veil, allowing us a tantalizing glimpse of the mysterious South-east wall. Through binoculars I focused upon a perfectly symmetrical fingernail summit. As I scanned down the dizzying sweep of red granite, a perfect line of fantasy began to imprint itself upon the well-featured wall.

---

* Serac. A column of glacial ice.

It was little wonder that Ladyfinger's face remained unclimbed until 1990.

Jim Beyer had gained some notoriety for his harrowing roped solo ascents on the crumbling sandstone of the Fisher Towers in Utah. With partner Pat McInerny, Beyer had embarked upon a faint line of weakness on the left side of this face. After two grueling and stormy days, McInerny went down, and Beyer continued alone to the top of the wall.

He had described the ascent to me over the phone, some months earlier. It had been a tale of stormy, multi-day bivouacs with minimal gear and hard climbing in worsening conditions. Being made of infinitely softer stuff, I started to wonder with gloom; what a place like this might do to a wuss like me.

Having turned an area of high pasture into a base camp of our liking, we set off to reconnoiter a higher camp the following morning, leaving Arif Ullah Baig to tend camp in our absence. A very caring and honest soul, Arif had overseen most major expeditions to the area, including Dave's earlier one. Upon returning to the camp later that day, we found Arif busy stoning sheep. We watched with some amusement as he hurtled after the flock, yelling, cursing and shot-putting large rocks at them. I didn't feel too sorry for the sheep, for in our absence they had eaten loads of our food and trampled our tents. One of the little bastards had even dared to tinkle on my clean thermal underwear.

My reverie was broken by a dull, resounding thud as one of Arif's rocks found its target. I suddenly felt saddened by the cruelty, but then remembered that Pakistan was still a developing country. People here didn't usually buy their dogs little chewy bones or send donkeys to obedience school. Welfare for animals usually equated to welfare for humans.

In the days that followed, we acclimated slowly while hauling gear and supplies up through the higher camps. In doing so, we gradually evolved into slightly fitter and more able human beings as we drew closer to our goal.

We finally arrived at a part of the world that resembled a kind of mildly destructive doomsday program. From the relative safety of the highest camp tucked away beneath an outcropping, we gazed despondently at nature's very own war zone.

Violent, powerful explosions reverberated across the valley, with rockfall to rival any Stinger missiles, Claymores, or cluster bombings. Rocks cascaded down from the neighboring peaks, bounced once or twice on the steep Ladyfinger glacier and pounded the nearby ridges and talus fields. A pungent odor of freshly ground granite permeated our nostrils.

"I'd rather saw my willy off with a nail file than go anywhere near that goddamn glacier," muttered James darkly.

We readily agreed.

Scouring the area for any alternatives to the deadly Ladyfinger glacier, we fixed our attentions upon a vast snow couloir to our immediate left that stretched up into God knows where.

Rockfall tumbled down this also, like runaway wheels in a grand prix race, but at much less than light speed. This bouncing, sliding cascade appeared to be eminently dodgeable. It suddenly seems like a fiendishly clever plan to me to blast up the couloir as far as possible and explore the crumbling rock ridge beyond. With any luck this might afford an aerial peek at the evil glacier and perhaps a different route up to the base of the wall.

Reality check. It was a sweltering afternoon, and the gully was alive with stone fall. Nevertheless, I departed the team and cramponed up into the eerie mouth of the gully. By staying close to the left wall, managed to make about six hundred feet of speedy and reasonably safe progress, dodging a few non-too-threatening 'sliders' along the way. Now I turned my attention toward crossing the slope and timed the intervals between rockfall while still trying to convince myself of the sanity of my project.

Picking my moment, I launched out onto the slope and began the 300 yard 'crab-crawl' to the other side. Halfway across, I dropped into a cavernous avalanche runnel that resembled a giant toboggan run. With senses peeking and feeling far too vulnerable, I crested the runnel and made it to the rocks without incident.

Sadly, I could make little headway up the crumbly rock and steep smatterings of rotten ice that might have taken me up to the crest of the ridge. Instead, nervous down climbing led back to the snow's edge, but the day had grown even warmer, and I bailed on the idea of trying to re-cross the slope. Caught up in my predicament, I was distracted for only a few seconds; then suddenly rooted to the spot when a wheel-sized rock spun by only a few feet from my head. I fled the gully and returned to camp with a lot more respect for this daunting, hostile environment.

Safely reunited, we chatted happily about the day and considered our not too numerous options. Gavin and I decided to make take another look at what I had just retreated from that day.

By leaving well before dawn, we thwarted the stone fall demons in the couloir and ambled up three pitches of loose rock on the other side, that soon landed us up at the knife-edged ridge above. Gavin was the first to arrive and I tried to read his facial expression…. Misery. We stood absolutely no chance of reaching any safer terrain beyond. Above us were many more extremely unstable 'slag heaps;' below us on the other side, only a bird's-eye view of the ear-shattering 'artillery range' below the snout of the glacier.

Hot and very thirsty, we had now managed to effectively trap ourselves, and would have to wait all day in the stifling heat before daring to rappel back down. Eventually, the shadows lengthened, and the cooler evening slowed down the constant rockfall, then finally, the long, uneasy rush-hour subsided, allowing us to spring onto the slope and tear back to camp in a flurry of glissading* and occasional faceplants.

While inhaling a voluminous breakfast the next day, we decided to attempt access to the Ladyfinger wall via a frontal assault beneath the lowest snout of the main glacier.

It was a grim artillery range that somehow came to be known as 'the showroom,' in view of all the various appliance-sized (e.g., toaster-sized, TV-sized and even Fridge-sized) missiles that ricocheted down from every direction. From a safe distance, we observed a slight lessening in the frequency of rockfall just as the air cooled down before nightfall. This would seem to be our only hope now and after an anxious scoping session through binoculars we decided to take the big risk.

With zero control on the outcome, it was a simple game of Russian Roulette, and that fearful loathing was visible on every face in our crew.

We dumped ludicrously heavy amounts of gear into our haul bags. Dave improved his overall target by adding two double portaledges, flysheets and some larger cams. In the gathering gloom we hoisted the loads and began cramponing across the lower delta of our favorite couloir. Soon we arrived at our moment of reckoning, as we cowered behind the last giant boulder before stepping into 'the showroom.'

Dead ahead lay the foreboding snout of the glacier. We would have to run the gauntlet for some 700 feet to reach the relative safety of a ratty old, fixed rope nestled between the ridge and the creaking towers of ice. All was dead quiet as we crept into the zone; feeling like tango dancers in a well-stocked minefield; braced for that terrifying 'something' that we all feared might happen.

---

* A controlled slide down a snow slope without skis, using an ice axe as a brake.

Then, right on cue, the silent air strike arrived from out of nowhere.

As the first salvos rained down, a large rock (toaster) missed my skull by mere feet. Rocks were exploding all around us with terrifying violence and debris ricocheted in all directions. This was followed by another (big screen TV, with surround sound) deadly wave of boulders that moved at light speed and pounded the ridge beyond.

Like synchronized swimmers, we turned in perfect unison and stampeded back to an open flat spot in the talus, a half a mile further down the long valley. Hearts pumping out pure adrenalin as we collapsed in the rocks like landed fish, gulping vainly for oxygen in the rarefied air. A storm rolled in and in no time, we were being lashed by torrential rain, hail and bolts of lightning. All we had with us were the two useless portaledges. Soaked to the skin, we made the best of things by rolling ourselves up inside the sturdy expedition flysheets and shivered away the night.

Dawn arrived; grey and dreary. I had just crawled out from my sodden mess to brew some tea when a salvo of rock came crashing down on our supposedly safe bivouac. Gavin was still sleeping but flew out of his bag as soon as the yelling began. A good-sized rock buried itself in the flysheet, right where his chest had been.

We were stunned beyond thought.

The bivouac had been hundreds of yards from the rocky slopes nearby, and we had just spent the entire night there. More than a little shaken, we baled all the way down to base camp, and obsessed about the possible existence of some malevolent mountain spirit. Something that simply didn't want us around.

Meadow camping was the required tonic for frayed nerves as the storm above raged on for two more days. We bantered on about where to take the expedition to next and sport climbing in Thailand became a hot favorite. Guilt presented a strong case for the defense however, and we winced at the thought of telling our friends back home that we didn't even make it to within a mile of the wall.

Chronically depressed, our endless discussions turned to compromise.

James and Gavin would muster up some more porters and head off to explore other remote corners of the Karakoram. Dave and I would remain; to plug away at the 'road to nowhere' couloir that I had snooped around in with Gavin. Because of the rockfall danger, we figured we'd tackle the approach and the climb in a single, alpine push.

As the last devastating powder avalanche teemed off the Ultar Mountains, Dave and I packed sparingly for an alpine assault on the Ladyfinger wall.

After dividing up the gear rack, two ropes and a few essentials, we only managed to cram in about five days food.

The approach via the 'never-ending' couloir took us a heart-rending three days.

Hiding our heads during daylight hours, we played unwilling audience to constant barrage of stone fall. At night, we would tiptoe like frightened mice; in a world blinkered by the thin beams of our headlamps. The steep gullies contained such hazards as shifting talus and ribbons of decomposing ice; but the biggest ordeal was not being able to see or dodge the occasional rocks that droned by us. We found ourselves sprinting between sheltered spots. Sometimes our legs would fail us and would drop to the ground like dying animals; waiting for the end to come.

Dawn on the third morning saw us perched on a rubble-strewn ridge looking down at the toe of the buttress that was still a mile away, but also seven hundred feet below. All around us, a panorama of unequalled beauty boggled the senses, but still we stood transfixed, soaking in the aura of our now attainable wall.

Spent and very hungry, we rattled down an exposed talus field and leapt onto the snowfield.

A quick sprint led over to the ledge system below Jim Beyer's route….and safety.

"I think we buried a bunch of gear over here," rasped Dave, pointing to a pile of boulders.

Dave and I dug deep and soon extricated a bunch of tattered ropes, some pitons and a bag containing the makings of a home-made portaledge.

After beating the ledge into something that might be slept on, we set about making a hot drink.

"Hey Dave, I'm not a bloater anymore. Look."

Any evidence of a beer belly had vanished, as our self-inflicted slim fast program took its toll. While desperately trying to conserve food, our daily ration consisted merely of one hot chocolate, two energy bars and a packet soup… between us. Food fantasies became a hot topic of conversation, and we spent a gut-rumbling night dreaming about some of our favorites.

It appeared that our meager rations might not allow for any drawn out first ascent epics, so we decided to tackle the Beyer route instead. The lower section was familiar ground to Dave from his attempt eight years earlier. He insisted on performing an all-day leading session, which got my full support, especially since the very first pitch offered technically hard climbing through an area of loose blocks. Dave tensioned off a piece stuffed behind one of those blocks, leaving me to ponder on the fact that any idea kind of self-rescue would be impossible from this position. He adeptly made it to easier ground and could then saunter up moderate rock to the base of the very furry three hundred feet of fixed rope that he'd abandoned years earlier.

Being forty pounds lighter, he offered to climb this too.

I almost climaxed with relief and spent a relaxing afternoon studying distant avalanches of falling rock, while ignoring Dave's plaintive whimperings.

Contentment was feeling warm and cozy, while lying on a creaky old portaledge amid towering Himalayan mountains. As the moon's luminescent light pierced the flysheet door, I gazed back at the stars and speculated upon the outcome of our little venture. We were progressing well, but the constant lack of food was making us both mentally slow and a little clumsy. As I stared at the moonlit face above, I tried to guess at the number of days it would take us to get up this prolonged big wall section and into the more alpine terrain higher up. Then, while Dave snored peacefully, I greedily licked dried soup crumbs from the empty packets out of the trash while wondering what real starvation might feel like.

Daylight finally broke and we moved bags, bodies and a fully intact portaledge 450 feet up the wall to our new high point. The next pitch was mine and turned out to be a cool, wandering crack in the 5.10 range. I was a little dizzy and breathless by the time I reached the foot of an imposing fifty-foot flake. As I peered deep into the shadowy depths of the five-inch crack, a very unwelcome ribbon of blue met my gaze; about ten feet away.

With slow dawning horror I realize that the whole thing was completely detached, tapering down to a hairline crack on its underbelly. I rejoined Dave at the belay, and we settled in for another night.

Another brilliant dawn and with little to cook, getting an early start had the both of us assembled on a sloping ledge off to one side of the giant flake. I cast a sideways glance at Dave and read the same thoughts of loathing. Instead of voicing the saner plan to leave this place, 'Death wish Dave' tensioned off the belay and dove for the crack instead. He latched it first time, and then proceeded to layback the serrated wafer edge, but not without kicking off a few chunks on his way past. Dark thoughts gave way to disbelief as he arrived on top, gasping loudly in the rarefied air.

Dave hauled up the aid rack and began to work the thin seam above. This was his first-time aid climbing, and I felt impelled to shout up a few pointers.

As he launched up onto his first piece, a birdbeak*, I cowered on the ledge and tried not to imagine the probable death fall, should that one piece pop out. Luckily, it didn't though and four hours later and with the pitch finally completed, I was left to marvel at an insane risk well taken.

The sun had long since disappeared from view when I launched into a section of hollow-sounding flakes. They offered some decent placements though, and so I managed to free climb up to a wildly exposed ledge. Finally, the upper face was in view.

My heart sank as I suddenly began to realize the total futility of it all. The much longed-for alpine ridge lay far beyond acres of seemingly featureless granite.

"At the rate we're going, we'll need another week to get through all this blank stuff.

Got any good ideas?"

"We only have half a day's food left." A dark pause. "I think we've blown it matey."

Dave had voiced an opinion that I was too chicken to make. A no food excuse sounded about as pathetic as they come. As I cleaned my pitch in the gathering gloom, I wanted nothing more than to crawl into the nearest hole and die.

Back on the portaledge, we polished off the last morsels of food and bedded down for another hungry night.

The following day, we descended to the base of the wall and wallowed in self-pity; while mulling over more immediate concerns; like being ravenous, foodless, and trapped.

There could be no retracing our steps, for with the snow line receding daily, rockfall on our marathon approach had been getting steadily worse. Our best chance of survival now would be to drop straight down the Ladyfinger glacier and run the gauntlet between pillars of ice and the rock ridge.

---

* a micro thin, hook shaped piton, used to ascend thin seams in the rock.

We would have to cross The Showroom, that loathsome shooting gallery; a funnel for rocks that rained down from all directions. The scene of our near tragedy and a most hated and feared place.

An insuppressible vision of fried eggs and heaping plates of French fries coagulated the decision-making process and we picked a completely random time of 4.45 pm for the big flee.

At that precise time, we bounded down onto the open slope. With one of us sprinting and the other scouting for falling rocks. We jumped a few crevasses and made a dash for the rocks.

Nothing came down.

Now we made three awkward rappels alongside the creaking serac walls and still nothing.

It was almost dark, and my headlamp had died many days earlier, but I had to keep moving regardless, into devilish piles of fresh debris.

Freezing sweat steamed off my body as I took off at a run and I was soon butt-sliding out of control across the rubble and kicking off minor landslides and avalanches. Suddenly I was up to my waist in a crevasse, with the booming sound of fast flowing water far below my feet. Renewed terror lent a new lease of life as I hurtled on down through the dreaded killing fields. Finally, in pitch blackness, I fumbled blindly across the last moraine and flung myself behind the nearest bombproof boulder.

The ecstasy of thwarting death was cut short by extreme uncertainty as I began to fear the worst for Dave. He was right behind me when I set off, but my worried shouts echoed back emptily, and I suddenly felt incredibly alone in this alien place.

Eventually, a light appeared; then big yells of delight as my bedraggled partner flopped down into the bunker. It was the happiest moment ever. We shared a cigarette and felt the thrill of anticipation for the world beyond.

The next morning, we wobbled unsteadily into a tent-less base camp. There was just a note from James and Gavin and a secret stash of food buried in the rocks. Absolutely brilliant. We ate like starving pigs and settled in with thoughts of staying the night to recoup some strength.

Then, like an apparition, Arif appeared. He had watched our arrival from a distant meadow and had hurried across to meet us.

Now he insisted on carrying an enormous pile of our gear, while shepherding us all the way back to the village.

Back at the hotel, James and Gavin had just returned from their mad wanderings, beating us back by a mere ten minutes. Elated, we shared amazing stories over staggering piles of food, before collapsing comatose into our beds.

We continued the marathon food-fest for three solid days. During this time, our locust-like appetites soon transformed us back to our original bloater status.

"I really want to maintain this present level of fitness," remarked James, who then cut loose with a window-rattling belch. We collapsed into hysterical laughter.

"Who's for coming back next year?" asked Dave.

All the hardship and fear of recent days had completely evaporated, replaced by a severe longing to be back climbing on the Ladyfinger wall again.

"Hell yes, but not in August. Let's try for a colder time of year." Gavin's sound reasoning was echoed by all of us.

Just after leaving Karimabad, we were invited to smoke aromatic herbs and oils.

Aside from their usual calming effect, they also imbued us with superhuman eating powers and I finally broke down and gorged on some meat.

Consequently, the scenic drive down the Karakoram was spent projectile vomiting at various cars, animals, and passersby.

Later on down the highway, as we entered another steep-sided gorge, I was still busy performing the very unsavory 'nasal jets.' As I gazed, trancelike at the rushing road below, I failed to witness the enormous landslide tumbling down the hillside towards us. Car-sized boulders caught on a wave of earth, came thumping down and completely closed the road behind us.

My comrades almost pooed their pants with fright.

"Looks like our lives just got marked down again," remarked Dave.

"Hmm. Who fancies a good bouldering session at Fontainebleau, in France?" queried Gavin.

"Moi. Absolutement, I replied"

A long approach to Lady Finger via the left
hand 'Road to Nowhere' Couloir.

Circuitous approach to Lady Finger

Melting snow for a brew after a prolonged, multi-night approach.

Feeling out the 50-foot detached flake

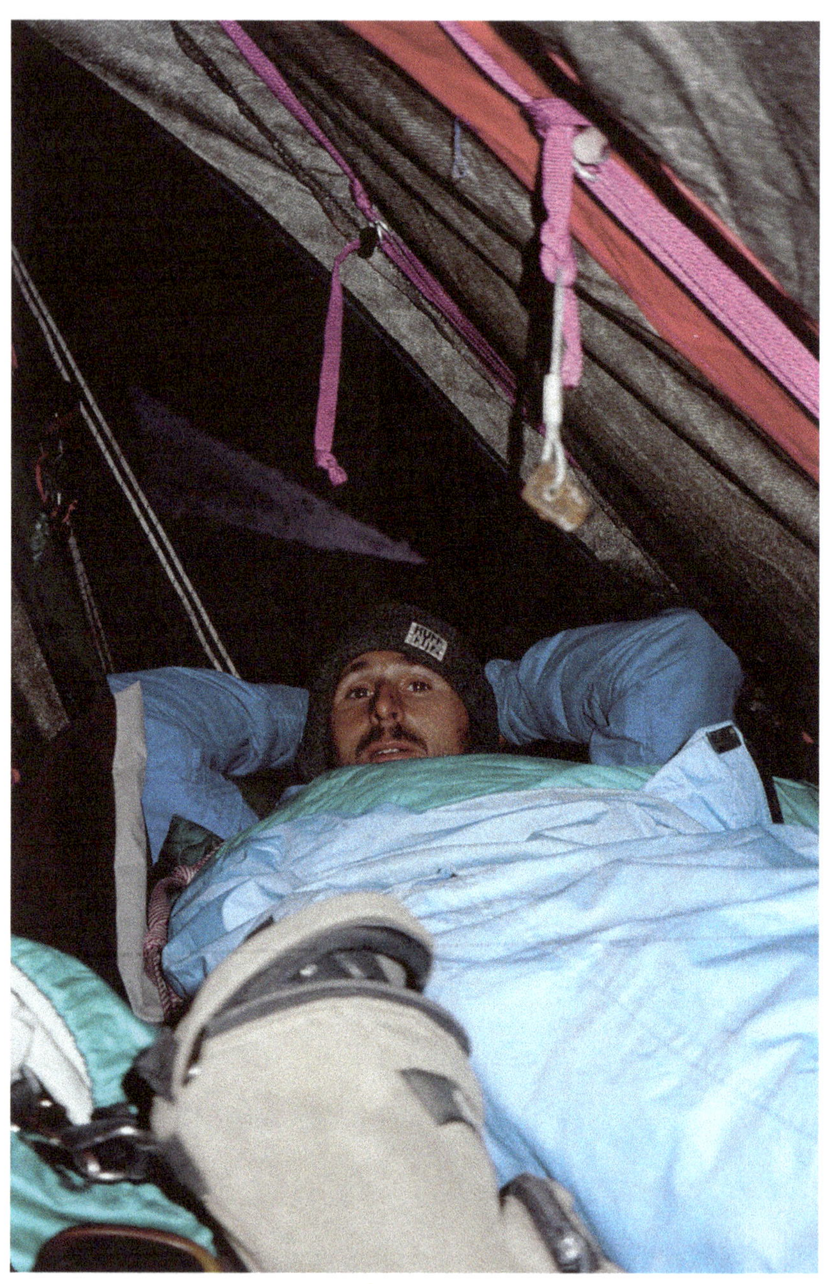

Dave ensconced on the rebuilt portaledge. Day two.

Chapter 9. La Cueva del Chupa Cabra (The Goat Sucker Cave).

"Is it better to out-monster the monster or to be quietly devoured?"
~Friedrich Nietzsche~

Just nine months after the Pakistan trip, a chance encounter, during a day of cragging in Boulder Canyon, set forth a chain of events that would ultimately whisk me away to a remote, uninhabited Caribbean Island named Mona. This was a truly magical place. Spectacular sea-cliffs encircled the land mass and towered above thundering ocean waves. A labyrinth of unexplored limestone caves stretched out across the entire ten-mile length of the island, like the honeycombed layer of a white chocolate cake. These tunnels could be accessed by 'natural windows,' situated fifty feet below the cliff's edge.

Mona Island is a wildlife preserve and is situated between Puerto Rico and the Dominican Republic.

Many fascinating legends surrounded these caves.

"In 1699, Captain Kidd was reputed to have spent about ten days here with a gold and silver laden prize, the Queddah Merchant, which was captured in the Indian Ocean. Kidd was later captured and hanged. The treasure was never found, and it had been suggested that it may be buried there." (The San Juan Star- April 28th, 1991).

We searched in vain for Kidd's treasure, just like so many others in centuries gone by. We did, however, turn up a wealth of incredible first ascents on Mona's steep ocean walls.

o0--0o

The vampire was close at hand. This vague unease seeped like a chilling mist into my subconscious, just moments before I willingly succumbed to the blissful caress of a warm feather sleeping bag. Sheer exhaustion washed over me. My tired gaze wandered without restraint across the surreal limestone roof and down the dizzying sweep of dolomitic rock to a relentless pounding ocean, far below.

Behind my solitary sleeping place in the dry dirt of the cave lay one of the eeriest places on earth; a contorted labyrinth of untrodden and unexplored passages that crossed the entire length of this long forgotten Caribbean Island.

Powerful moonlight bounced back from a silvery sea and coated the cavern walls in rich mercury. I peered nervously beyond the translucent light and into the shadowy maze of calcite columns that melted into inky blackness. So easy to get lost in there. Such a horrible way to die; wandering helplessly, until your light fails you and then waiting all alone; crying and screaming in the darkness; praying for madness to take over. I shuddered at the thought, sensing perhaps that something was not quite right with this place. Suddenly, a sharp intake of breath as I caught sight of the creature lying prostrate in the dirt only twenty feet away from me. Her arms were outstretched in a crucifix position and her eyes were closed. Why hadn't I noticed her earlier? In a twilight state between dream life and complete wakefulness, I stared transfixed. Could this be the vampire known as, 'Chupacabra,' (goat sucker) the bloodsucking monster known and feared by people throughout Mexico and the Caribbean? I felt very at ease with her sleeping so close by and became enraptured by her riveting beauty; her sleeping face. Utterly fascinated, my attention was drawn towards those closed eyes. Suddenly, the eyes flicked wide open as she emitted a hideous catlike snarl. In a flash she hurtled through the air towards me, her long fingers curled like talons.

I screamed as the nightmare broke, leaving me sitting bolt upright, soaked in sweat, and gasping for breath.

The moon had left the cave window, and it was much darker now. Labored breathing soon subsided, but sleep had deserted me and so I lay back, closed my eyes and tried to retrace the series of events that led me to visit this fairytale island.

As a world class climber, Craig Luebben's enthusiasm for the sport was quite unique. He not only designed and manufactured climbing gear but was also a noted mountain guide. When time allowed, he had also found time to make his mark as a gifted author and climbing photographer.

I first met him while climbing up in Boulder Canyon. We introduced and chatted amicably about our respective climbing adventures in faraway lands. He talked passionately about incredible sea-cliff climbing on various Caribbean islands. One of these islands was Cayman Brac. According to Craig, the place had stunning potential for first ascents, but had already been 'colonized' by an ex-girlfriend along with her fiancée. Miffed by this, Craig had set out to try to discover his very own island paradise.

He had immediately enlisted the support of one of his regular climbing partners, Skip Harper. The two of them had begun their quest by poring over maps, charts, and info on a whole flotilla of seldom visited Caribbean islands. This was how they came to set the dream in motion; by discovering Mona Island, an inaccessible island fortress and wildlife sanctuary, poised squarely in the middle of the notorious Mona Passage, requiring a vulnerable fifty-mile crossing from tourist beach towns on either Puerto Rico or the Dominican Republic.

The chance discovery of the words, "200' high sea-cliffs," in a travel guide prompted an immediate exploration. With all the practiced nonchalance of a seasoned Vegas gambler, Craig mounted his first expedition to one of the world's premier sea-cliff climbing areas.

I listened in awe as Craig embellished wildly upon all the marvels of Mona Island. Suddenly, I could not believe my ears for now he invited me, a total stranger, to go back with him. I recounted a very similar episode to this many years earlier when I had happened upon a brief passage in a biographical work by the great explorer, John Muir.

Regarding a fiord in Southeast Alaska, he wrote something like: "An untraveled world of unsurpassed beauty, not unlike a giant Yosemite by the ocean."

That was all I needed to hear. In a blind, pioneering frenzy, I hauled a trailer loaded with sea kayaks 2500 miles up to Alaska. I had then chartered a very expensive fishing boat to take us in, but discovered nothing but seeping walls of grass, set amongst a backdrop of towering icebergs. Breathtaking beyond belief, but totally unclimbable.

Now I was thinking that I should probably have known a whole lot better as Craig and I shook hands and committed to the expedition.

"Don't worry about a thing, Strappo. Mona will blow your mind when you see it," chirped Craig.

Flying into San Juan, Puerto Rico, several months later, I was just about speechless with anticipation.

Craig had booked us into a palatial beachside hotel, but when I quizzed him about this monumental extravagance, he recalled a tale of his previous visit when, amid the all-knowing smiles of the hotel staff, he had accidentally booked them into an hourly 'motel,' replete with vibrating beds and overhead mirrors.

"You should have seen the looks we got when the three of us left the place the following day."

The next morning, I was buried up to my nipples in a sumptuous feather bed and more than ready to veto any further escapades on or around cold mountains.

After breakfast, Craig introduced me to the third team member; Rossano Boscarino. A keen athlete, Rossano always had a mischievous glint in his eye. He had been instrumental in introducing the sport of climbing to Puerto Rico and had pioneered many routes on the local limestone crags. He also ran a successful cave guiding company and had graciously consented to use us as guinea pigs; by guiding us through a seldom visited system of passages, five hundred feet below the earth.

Grinning with maniacal intent, Rossano navigated the 'Adventuras Tierra Adentro' bus up the winding dirt roads and into the jungle clearing. A dozen or so clients were disgorged and proceeded to wander around the clearing like Alzheimic penguins. Twenty minutes later, we were all transformed into replica Navy Seals; fully kitted up with helmets, caving lamps, life preservers and wet suits. After a short slog through the forest, we arrived at the brink of an enormous sinkhole. I caught sight of the fixed line that ran diagonally down into a jungle canopy far below and my neck hairs tingled at the thought of committing to such a gripping void.

"Just clip yourselves into the pulley system and we'll send you down the line," offered Rossano cheerfully. Feeling a little out of our depth, Craig and I glanced at each other nervously, then at the teenage rope handlers, then at Rossano. Not wishing to lose face in front of the less experienced clients we duly clipped into the double pulley and off we went. With a nervous lump in my throat, I distracted myself by sliding a Teva sandal down the vine-clad wall prior to shoving off into the void. In doing so, I inadvertently flattened the home of some house-proud and very aggressive wasps.

"Rapido, Rapido," we yelled, suddenly finding ourselves swatting furiously but helplessly as the angry cloud of stingers found their target.

A little while later, we were all assembled by the river's edge, deep inside the sinkhole.

Rossano broke out some antihistamine and a soak in the clear river water soon helped to ease our dozen or so stings.

Soon we were meandering along in the river's edge as it became swallowed up by the mouth of a gigantic cave. Then we witnessed a truly surreal sight as a rippling black carpet of bats commuted to and fro across the cavern roof in search of their daily insect feast. One by one, we lay back in our life preservers and let the river gently carry us on an incredible journey, through the dark caves and out into a dappled, sunlit rainforest. A green and yellow world of pristine beauty.

In the days to come, we set about the formidable task of trying to find a boat ride out to Mona Island. No small feat this, for none of the skippers that we talked to had the slightest inclination to venture anywhere near the notorious Mona Passage. To make matters worse, very few boats were licensed to carry passengers and fewer still could withstand the huge thirty-foot swells and swift currents.

Unbearable delays. Craig and I wiled away the time exploring various limestone crags and establishing some decent first ascents, but we were almost losing our minds with frustration. To be this close to unraveling the mysteries of Mona, but then having to get on a plane and fly home. Extreme depression set in, and I felt like screaming. With only a week remaining, we decided to gamble it all and loaded Rossano's truck almost to bursting point. Poring over endless equipment lists, we packed and slaved through the night, finally catching an hour's sleep before the pre-dawn race across the island to Puerto Real. As the bustling beach town churned into life, we ate breakfast and caroused the dive shops, but without any luck whatsoever. Dejected, Craig and I moped around the bleak shanties down by the harbor. Then a sharp yell pierced the air as Rossano sprinted through the village towards us, flapping his arms in a very excited manner. "We've got one! We've got one!

Craig and I scurried after him and arrived in time to witness the transaction. All a little shady this; involving huge wads of hard cash, and not unlike some inner-city crack deal.

An hour later, our heaps of equipment, food and forty gallons of water were stowed below, and we scrabbled for the best seats on deck. Dangerously overexcited, we broke out one of the bottles of Bacardi and began to chug.

As we cast off from the dock, the skipper punched the throttle and aimed the bow inexorably in the direction of Mona. My thoughts returned once again to the legendary 'Chupa Cabra.' As another large belt of Puerto Rican rum washed down my throat.

Well, I mused. If that scary ass goatsucker sucks any of my blood, then he'll probably end up in the Betty Ford Clinic with the D. T's.

"Land Ho!" ...I slurred. Four roller coaster hours had skated by, and right there, between ominous dark clouds and a somber ocean, a tabletop island rose dramatically to meet us at the outermost edge of the world. The boat's engines screamed as she crested another wave wall and started to plunge into the next deep trough.

Soon we were grinning like complete idiots as the island revealed some of her finer features; and we beheld fantastic rock walls and caves big enough to hide a ship. We were closing in now, and dead ahead we spied our access beach; but the sudden roaring of a nearby reef sent a jolt of fear through me. The skipper carefully negotiated the fifty-foot-wide channel, past a maelstrom of crashing breakers and the remnants of an old freighter.

Ashen faced and sober, we arrived at the jetty and ferried the supplies over to a secluded beach site.

Over dinner, Craig spoke of his first visit to the island. The team had consisted of five strong and very able climbers. Accompanying Craig were Leslie Barber, Tom Kelly, Skip Harper and George Bracksieck. They had established some difficult routes on the cave walls right behind our beach camp and then had explored much of the ten miles of virgin sea cliffs.

It was only on the last day of their trip that they took the plunge and rappelled down towards the crashing breakers that pounded the island relentlessly.

"A short forty-foot rappel off the cliff top lands you at a ledge,' explained Craig. "The main cliff drops down for another 200 feet to the sea below. From this ledge, it is possible to squeeze through a narrow fissure in the rock and access a complex labyrinth of cave passages.

Many of these tunnels appear to lead to these wild, natural windows that look back out across the sea.

With overhanging rock above the windows, access would be difficult at best. If we could find a way through the cave passages to any of these windows, we could rappel out of them to a hanging stance above the crashing waves…and then climb back up. Man, it would be a blast."

"You're completely out of your gourd," I reply, only half joking.

Craig paused, feigning a look of hurt.

"We never had time to explore those caves. Do you fancy hiking over there right now and taking a look? We could haul some gear over there and save ourselves a bunch of work in the morning."

At around midnight, Craig and I set off up the single, steep road that left the beach and sliced through impenetrable cactus jungle for two and a half miles, to terminate at a long-abandoned lighthouse. With the sounds of creaking and the slamming of rusted old iron shutters blowing in the breeze, the place was unimaginably eerie in the dead of night.

Blinkered by the narrow beams of our headlamps, we followed a faint meandering trail out to the cliff's edge where we donned harnesses, uncoiled ropes and prepared to descend. My heart was in my mouth as I leaned out on the rope and began to rappel down into the inky blackness.

The booming thunder of crashing waves far below seemed to reverberate through the core of the island. Forty feet down and sure enough, I landed at a spacious ledge. We dumped the loads and Craig pointed to a narrow slit in the rock.

"Check this out," he beamed and promptly disappeared into the crevice. I followed cautiously, totally unprepared for the scene that greeted me, as I entered a world of complete silence, a magical maze of wild stalagmite columns and crystal pools. After only a few minutes of careful wandering, we caught sight of a faint glimmer of moonlight and suddenly found ourselves at one of the windows that looked out onto a wild sea.

"This is total paradise," I whispered, numbed in the face of such haunting beauty.

We lingered late into the night, before retracing our long journey back up to the cliff top and across the island, arriving at our beach camp shortly before dawn with a heartfelt desire for rest.

Rossano was up early. Eager for action, he strutted about camp like a budgie in heat.

A later start than we would have wished for had us re-hiking the island road in the shimmering haze of noontime heat.

A truly idyllic afternoon was spent exploring the caves, locating windows, and then inspecting vast expanses of rock below them, occasionally spinning like a spider near the end of the rappel rope. The base of the wall was always severely undercut and right beneath me, booming waves pounded the island, as I counted the number of seconds before these giant waves returned to the sea.

A close inspection of the rock revealed all manner of edges and pockets, allowing for some phenomenal climbing. I took a mental note of a whole slew of 'must do' lines up the cliffs and returned to the cave windows practically choking on my own enthusiasm. Back at camp later that night, we eagerly compared notes on all that we'd seen while noisily stuffing our faces.

Dinner consisted of any can of food that came to hand, speedily opened, and quickly downed in two or three gulps.

Thoroughly exhausted and feeling more than a little top-heavy, I collapsed inside my tent and passed out in seconds, but a loud commotion from outside soon had me resurfacing from deep sleep.

"Strappo, Strappo, wake up. I think a boat has just gone down on the reef!"

Rossano and Craig had just heard an ominous foghorn in the darkness, and then from behind the reef, a red distress light had suddenly disappeared. Not at all good.

A blustery wind picked up as my friends took off at a sprint to summon help from two rangers who were stationed at Sardinero, some seven miles across the island. I stood watch at the end of the narrow pier; shining my flashlight into the water while waiting for the bodies to start floating ashore and hating myself for being unable to help. The hours seem to drag like days. Suddenly the dimmest outline of a boat reappeared and wove back and forth behind the reef. Very strange indeed. But even weirder still were the two shotgun-toting rangers who came blazing down the beach in their jazzed-up Baja style 4x4 truck. They flashed the vessel repeatedly, until she finally responded with that same blazing red beacon of light followed by frenzied radio message. Rossano informed us that we had just managed to piss off the Coast Guard. It seemed they had been on some covert mission to track down drug-runners and illegal aliens; and our song and dance with radios and flashlights had blown it for them.

We shed our worried looks and turned in for what was left of the night, greatly relieved that nothing bad had happened.

Over the next few days, we worked ourselves hard, humping ropes and gear to windows further inside the labyrinth rappelling down onto other, even crazier-looking sea walls.

We spent one wild afternoon roaming around in the maze of caves, working our way inland, while casually hunting for long lost treasure. Getting lost in here was absolutely not an option, so we lay down a life preserving trail composed of large, papery leaves collected from our beach camp. One leaf was laid down every twenty feet, with the base of the stem pointing to the way out.

After thirty minutes of crouching and stooping, Craig discovered an ancient wooden staff, lying half-buried in the dirt. We left it undisturbed though, and pressed on, thoroughly amazed that someone could have made it in here before us.

Soon, the passages grew more numerous and started to fan out in every direction with an alarming level of complexity.

"It might take an army three lifetimes to cover every passage in here," exclaimed Craig.

How true. There seemed to be no reason to keep pressing on, so instead, we retraced our steps and re-bagged our leaves. A couple of these precious marker leaves were accidentally kicked or trampled on during the journey back, and momentary panic crept in as the way to safety was momentarily lost. With the onset of group claustrophobia and resultant hysteria, the appearance of the first 'window-framed' patch of daylight was viewed with the same reverence as a visitation from God.

We continued our sea cliff reconnaissance the following day and scoped out a tally of ten possible new lines of varying difficulty. The real work began that morning, and while still reveling in our dramatic surroundings, the following days took on a much more serious air. The routes were rigorously inspected and sneakily bolted. Complete exhaustion and serious dehydration stalked us like a shadow and any small mistake could spell disaster. Ropes started to fray badly on the razor-sharp limestone below the windows. Craig solved this problem by producing some small sections of carpet to pad the offending areas and all was well.

By the end of day four, all the routes were ready to be climbed cleanly. A practice known as redpointing- whereby the rope is used only as a safeguard in the event of a fall and the climber must ascend the rock using mere fingertips and the sticky rubber tips of a pair of modern rock shoes.

Expectations were high and with the trip drawing to a close, I opted to spend the night alone up in the caves and save myself a long morning slog. However, the absolute quietness was almost stifling after living with the constant booming surf. I let the numbness wash over me, but as I drifted off into a womb-like sleep, the stillness was broken by the unmistakable sound of something scratching across the cave floor towards me.

Oh my god, it's the Chupa Cabra!

My hands trembled as I fumbled in the pitch dark for the flashlight and a shaking beam of light suddenly landed on a large plate-sized crab hovering at the end of my sleeping bag. He was outraged at my intrusion into his domain and waved his pincers at me in a menacing fashion. I smiled. "What on earth are you doing here?" I voiced the question out loud to him but indifferent to me, he plodded away into the darkness.

Mona. Always a place of mysteries. I puzzled as to why a crab would choose to live three miles from a beach and 250 feet above the sea, then pondered the darker notion that maybe he could be a scout to some vast army of man-eating crabs that lurked deep inside the maze.

The weight of solitude fueled a rampant imagination and it only seemed like moments later when I first noticed the outstretched vampire that was keeping me company in the shadows. Horrific, Faustian nightmares plagued my every move as I plowed through a night of broken, fitful dreams.

By morning, all the terrors of the night had already slithered quietly away. A blazing shaft of tangerine sunlight etched the cave wall in blood orange bronze as I cut loose with a loud, bleary-eyed yawn. As I stretched out my aching back, the hideous nightmare resurfaced. Wild eyes darted furtively back into the shadows, seeking out the unwelcome form of a sleeping woman, but all was calm, and my thoughts returned to the day at hand.

Throat moisture had long since departed for more appreciative body areas, but I attempted to force a couple of breakfast bars down anyway, and then will my battered carcass to vacate the sleeping bag. Deep in the maze, I caught the distant murmur of voices; then bobbing flashlights heralded the arrival of Craig and Rossano.

"Come on, 'Sluggo,' it's showtime. Let's get to work."

An hour later, we were hanging from the same solid anchor; poised just out of reach of the roaring, fifty-foot waves.

We stared nervously at an immaculate bulging wall of creamy fossilized rock, stretching all the way up to the cave window, far above us.

"You want to give it a go Craig?" A brief pause, then a smile.

"Hell, why not?" And off he went, launching himself into a dynamic series of arm-pumping power moves, interspersed with the odd bucket hold. Amid shrieks of delight, Craig freed the climb and pulled himself back into the cave window then anchored himself to the oversized calcite column just inside.

Now it was my turn.

Blessed with the security of an overhead rope, I risked some even more unlikely moves, soon joining our intrepid leader in his cave.

As I tended to the rope, Craig shot spectacular footage as Rossano teetered above the rolling waves that slammed the wall below. I caught sight of a large sea turtle, idly floating on the surface and watching us intently.

In a miracle of dogged perseverance, we managed to redpoint all ten of our routes in a day-long flurry of manic, exhausted, and dangerously thirsty activity.

As nighttime closed in around us, we hauled the last bag of climbing gear back through the labyrinth and up to the cliff top. The dying rays of a cherry sun set the island aglow as we crouched giddily near the edge; to take a last fond look down at the monolithic sea walls below. We stayed awhile, drinking in the keen salt air and the utter loneliness of this vast ocean. Storms were building not too far out to sea, so we quickly hoisted our bulging packs and began a delirious but elated stagger towards the torrential drenching rain that awaited us, back towards the violent sheet lightning, back to our beach haven and then finally, to oblivion.

Photo credit. Craig Luebben

Some nice, pocketed limestone. One of the larger cave
windows behind. Photo credit. Craig Luebben

Playing nosy neighbor in a cave Window.
Photo credit. Craig Luebben

Rappelling in to start the day

Rossano Boscarino working it! Photo credit. Craig Luebben

Chapter 10. Tricky Dicky

"Pain is temporary. Quitting lasts forever."
  ~Lance Armstrong~

Upon returning to Boulder after such a deliriously fun and epic Caribbean adventure, it was time to switch gears and prepare for a much more serious escapade. I had allowed myself to be talked in to attempting the South Face of Mt Dickey on the Ruth glacier in Alaska. Weighing in as one of the tallest rock walls in the world, this monster excursion would require a huge level of commitment, tenacity, and grit.

First, we would have to drive 3200 miles up to Anchorage, where we would meet the rest of the team, then load up with supplies, before hitting the final 120 miles north to the historic mining town of Talkeetna. This town was also the staging area for the thousand plus climbers wishing to attempt Denali (Mount McKinley), each year.

We had booked a flight into the Ruth glacier, which would be our home for the upcoming three weeks.

After a mere twenty-four hours to decompress from the Mona trip, I was bundled into Steve Quinlan's transit van and off we sped. Steve was a mildly stoic and comic minded seasonal mountain guide and longtime friend. We had shared many epic adventures together, mainly on Utah's desert sandstone towers and in the Black Canyon of the Gunnison.

The woman riding shotgun with us was Lynne Romano. Lynne was eager to see Alaska and reunite with an old friend; Little Diane, who lived up in Anchorage.

Steve had attempted the South face of Dickey ten years earlier with a legend in the climbing world; Mugs Stump. Mugs was one of the all-time greats in Alaskan alpine climbing. Sadly, he was killed in a crevasse fall while descending the South Buttress of Denali with a couple of clients. The loss of Mugs was an enormous blow to the climbing community. What I would soon learn from Steve gave me more than a little pause for thought. Not only was I driving to Alaska with Mugs' old climbing partner to retry their route, but we were also traveling in Mugs' van, and I was sitting right next to Mugs' girlfriend! I felt a little uneasy and not at all worthy to be daring to tread in the footsteps of such greatness, Lynne soon turned out to be a warm and spirited companion during the trip and we all became great friends.

Our route followed the magnificent but isolated Stuart Cassiar highway along the western side of British Columbia. This 544 mile stretch of forest lined dirt roads offered unrivaled views of distant, snowcapped coastal peaks and mist enshrouded river valleys and lakes. This was a far cry from Mona Island, where I'd been sweltering my buns off under a fierce, tropical sun just a few days earlier, but my blood soon thickened as I quickly readjusted to the much cooler weather.

Eventually, we rolled up to Diane's house in Anchorage feeling very travel weary after a nonstop, three-day drive. Her home was quite upscale and was nestled in the tranquil backstreets on the edge of town near the deep, dark forest. After a lively evening, I set up my tent on the neatly manicured lawn out in her front yard. She had mentioned that a mama moose had just delivered a calf nearby and warned me not to stray too far from my tent. More than happy to comply, I dove deep into my down sleeping bag, but sleep eluded me, for I could still feel the thrum of the van's motor and its constant swaying motion, as I lay awake well into the night.

Alaska: the land of the midnight sun lived up to its name, for outside the tent walls in the 3am twilight, I could make out the not-too-distant buzz of a circular saw, followed by the pop, pop of a nail gun. Someone was actually framing a house nearby! Then came the buzz of a chainsaw from the opposite direction, then a dirt bike. It seemed like these people just never ever slept!

The next morning, we bade Diane and Lynne farewell and drove off in search of some strong coffee, only to realize that Anchorage seemed to have more coffee shops per acre than anywhere else. Perhaps this might help to explain all those nocturnal goings on.

Soon, it was time to head off to the airport and swoop our other two members of the team. Noel Craine and Jimmy Surette. These were a couple of top notch, bad ass expedition climbers.

In the preceding four years, Noel had played an integral part in two successful expeditions to world renowned mountain big walls. In early 1992, came the first and all British ascent of the East face Of the Central Tower of Paine in Patagonia with Paul Pritchard, Simon Yates, and Sean smith. Then on June 10th, 1994, along with our host; Steve Quinlan, they climbed the extremely remote; West face of the North Tower of Mount Asgard, on Baffin Island in the Canadian Arctic. This team comprised, Jordi Tosas, Paul Pritchard, Keith Jones, and Simon Yates.

A tall, slightly unkempt, and well-spoken rock climber, Noel had winched me up more than a couple of harder climbs back in North Wales in recent years.

As a successful alpinist and film producer, Jimmy Surette's resume detailed a prolific hit list of cutting-edge climbs worldwide; places as far afield as; Nepal, Patagonia, Pakistan, Peru, Kyrgyzstan, and Yosemite to name but just a few. Noel and Jimmy would be attempting a big unclimbed line on the imposing Mount Barrille, just to the north of Mount Dickey.

Following a round of wildly enthusiastic hugs and handshakes, we headed off in search of one of the larger superstores and soon had the van loaded to the roof with enough food and supplies to survive at least three weeks on the Ruth glacier and hopefully many days on our respective walls too.

After a scenic, two-hour drive northwards along the Glenn highway, we arrived in the bustling mountain town of Talkeetna. First, we scouted out a secluded pull-off for the van on the outskirts of town and then sidled down main street and into the historic Fairview Inn, where we settled in for a few pints and some mission briefing. Steve called the airfield and learned to his dismay that unsettled weather conditions might preclude any chance of a flight into the Ruth glacier that day and so, enlivened by aforementioned pints, he set about trying to hunt down some legendary Matanuska Thunderfuck marijuana instead, just in case 'somebody' in the group needed it.

A bit later on, all plans for a leisurely afternoon of weed smoking quickly evaporated, as word reached us that the gods had favored our expedition with a decent weather window and that we should make haste to the airfield immediately.

Our wheel and ski equipped bush plane was quite the specialized little rig, with both fat rubber tires for tarmac and a pair of broad, heavy-duty skis for glacier landings, allowing for relatively smooth and graceful touchdowns upon all but the worst snow or ice conditions.

The one-hour flight into the Ruth glacier was nothing short of mind-blowing.

As we drew closer towards the unmistakable profile of Denali, the clouds unveiled and a misty, river strewn tundra gave way to a giant, upwelling of icefields, agape with a daunting web of crevasses and sharp ice ridges.

Soon we were gazing down at some of Alaska's most impressive high mountain walls, rising up from beyond the fringe of a thirty mile long, seemingly inhospitable glacier. The pilot of our cramped little Cessna eased back on the throttle, and we began to lose height as we neared our destination. A nervous unease crept in as I watched the snowfield below come racing towards us; muscles tensing, bracing for a hard landing then the roar of the engine in deceleration as we touched down and ground to an abrupt and uneventful halt.

We exited the aircraft and spun around in awe of our surroundings, having been set down smack in the middle of the two-mile-wide glacier and now in close proximity to Dickey and Barrille, with their immense walls of dark rock, steep gullies and chaotic hanging snowfields. Steve pointed out the line that he'd tried with Mugs years earlier.

An enticing pillar of darker rock rose up from a smaller side glacier nearby. They had climbed this nine-hundred-foot monolith to some welcome ledges on top but had been unable to move onto the giant face above due to a constant cascade of falling rocks.

I gazed worryingly at the distant skyline of our intended rock wall, then at the vast, sweeping snowfield above and tried to imagine myself up there, lost in its immensity and with every chance of falling victim to a whole slew of potential disasters.

Just an attack of preflight jitters, I hoped.

No time for wimpish distractions, for there was a campsite to erect and the weather still seemed to be holding.

We grabbed our two hefty snow shovels and began carving out level, sheltered site beneath the surface snowpack for our oversized, base camp dome tent. After packing down sufficient blocks of snow to create a functional wind break around it, we set about building four more sites to house our individual tents, then finally, a deep poo hole; excavated safely away from base camp, to serve as our not overly private latrine.

Finally, with food and equipment stashed and dinner bubbling away noisily, we stepped outside to take stock of our surroundings once again. It was only early June, and the Ruth was still sporting a deep blanket of snow, so luckily, we weren't seeing too many exposed crevasses between our camp and the wall. Being so completely alone on this vast glacier added weight to the all-consuming silence around us.

Suddenly, the hint of a silvery crystalline full moon peeked out from beyond the distant peaks and soon rose in perfect clarity, to coat the neighboring peaks in rich, mercurial light.

Being hugely travel weary and weedless, my comrades turned in for an early night, leaving me to bask in the absolute stillness and desolation.

It was gone eleven o'clock at night and I could still make out far away features in perfect detail. With the moon blazing down and being far too amped to even consider turning in, I loaded up my haulbag with ropes and as much climbing hardware as I could physically carry; strapped on my mountaineering skis and set off in the direction of the dark pillar.

Skiing alone at night and unroped, across a big Alaskan glacier was just asking for trouble.

"But it all looked so doable. I could always turn back if things started getting dicey," I reasoned to myself.

Relying on blind luck just wouldn't cut it though, so I delicately probed anything resembling a snow-covered crevasse. After a couple of mini frights and some careful backtracking, I managed to break a relatively safe ski trail into the side glacier and up to a snow free boulder near the base of the wall. I dumped the bag and sat for a while; feeling blessed and empowered to be perched so high above the vast and silent world below me.

With ski tracks to follow, I made it back down to camp in double quick time, to the gentle sound of soft snoring emanating from the various tents. The moon was still up and after my solo ski run, I was now infinitely more amped up than before.

I feverishly pondered on what other mischief I could get into; then a thought hit me.

If a couple of my colleagues hadn't managed to secure any of the revered 'Matanuska Thunderfuck, then... maybe we could flag down a passing plane a try to score some.

Without much in the way of thought or reason, I began to stomp out a message in the snow near camp with my skis, which read, SMOKING MATERIALS? Each letter was over ten feet long and I took pride in my wording as I hopped from letter to letter on the shimmering nighttime snowscape.

I awoke the next morning to the steady drone of overhead ski planes ferrying tourists and climbers in towards the Ruth Amphitheater, a very popular landing site below Denali. Striding into the dome tent, I proudly announced we might receive an air drop of marijuana from a passing plane at any minute. I took my friends outside and showed them my handiwork. They stared at the lettering in disbelief and then back at me, with a look of genuine concern; either for my failing sanity or the trouble that we might bring down upon ourselves; I'm not sure which.

Suddenly, the crackle of a call coming in on our walkie talkie back in the tent had us scurrying back to intercept it.

"Glacier base camp, glacier base camp. Do you copy? Over."

"Come in. Over!"

I informed the pilot that it wasn't looking very green down here. He laughed and wished us all the best of luck and then signed off. With the dawning realization that the National Park Service monitored all radio calls in case of an emergency, I began to feel extremely stupid, not to mention me having created a huge eyesore for all to see. Dripping with guilt, I spent one solid hour stomping out the sign with my skis before we could turn our attentions back to climbing again.

That afternoon, Steve and I ferried in more loads to the base of Mt Dickey, while Noel and Jimmy skied into the base of Mt Barrille to reconnoiter their line on the east face.

I was happy that Steve and I were roped together this time after my double whammy of stupidity the night before. Even so, the chances of just one climber rescuing another were remote at best, especially if one is dangling in space inside the depths of a bitterly cold crevasse. The thought of poor Mug's demise struck home more so now than ever before.

After dumping our loads on top of the boulder, we scoped out the dark pillar with binoculars, focusing on a continuous system of thin cracks shooting straight up the middle.

My mood of foreboding vanished and now I was raring to go. The weather was still behaving beautifully and so it was decided. We would vacate flat ground first thing the following morning.

Like overexcited school kids we skied jubilantly back to the tent, only to discover two very despondent faces in deep scowl mode. We learned that Noel and Jimmy had approached the base of their wall, only to discover a system of giant, yawning crevasses; one being over forty feet wide; that separated the level glacier from the steepening rock wall above. They had attempted every means possible to safely navigate this formidable 'Bergschrund,' but nothing had worked. Trying to cheer them up didn't seem to work either, but after a few shots of single malt whiskey and some more serious debate, it was decreed that they would head back the following morning for 'just one more look.'

Another pristine morning saw Steve and I parking our skis by the boulder cache and repacking our two bulbous haulbags with food, water and a double portaledge in preparation for our climb. Steve led off from the ground and made good time on the initial cracks, then I led the second pitch, which I found to be straightforward free climbing, mixed in with short sections of aid.

This was little old me, climbing a big wall in Alaska, just like one of those true climbing legends that I'd read so much about.

The thought thrilled me to no end.

Much later that evening we were sprawled out in the portaledge with the zipper cracked in the extra heavy-duty flysheet to release the steam from a hearty meal of pasta and various dehydrated offerings. We had climbed about four hundred feet that day. The weather was still on our side and now the stars were coming out in force.

Halfway through the next day's climbing, a call came in on the radio. It was Noel.

"We've had it with this place. Both of us were dead set on Barrille and now we don't feel like trying anything else out here. We called in a plane and will wait for you in Talkeetna. Please be careful up there."

Sure enough, about an hour later, we watched from far away as a small ski plane landed at the camp. The recent hot weather had turned the surface snow on the glacier into slush, so the pilot had to create his own runway by 'driving' the plane back and forth multiple times, until the surface would allow for a clean take off. Finally, everything was loaded, and two tiny specks boarded the plane. Even from so far away, we could hear the engine scream as she sought to free herself from the glutinous snow and fly like a bird again. One of the loneliest moments ever was watching that tiny plane disappear towards the horizon and the distant engine sound fade into absolute silence.

Things got a little trickier, but not by much. By the end of day three we had a rope fixed to within easy, spitting distance of the top of the pillar, but the blue skies gradually faded to grey, and a cutting wind quickly sought out chinks in our layers of warm clothing. Sensing the onset of a real storm, we set up our hanging camp early and bedded in for what was left of the day.

A voracious Alaskan blizzard raged all around us for the next four days.

As chunks of ice cascaded down around us and with some even bouncing painfully off our flysheet, we were feeling far too exposed and vulnerable. If only for peace of mind, we quickly took to living and sleeping with our helmets on.

The rope that we had fixed on the pitch above became a curtain of icicles and with visibility down to just twenty or so feet, we hunkered down, oblivious to the constant rattle as a gusting wind constantly buffeted our flysheet.

Luckily, I had thrown a couple of paperback books into the haulbag before leaving. Unfortunately, they were both stories about suffering and deprivation, which didn't do much to appease our current predicament. Ernest Shackleton's 'Endurance' told a true tale of shipwreck and starvation in the Southern Ocean, with a subsequent sixteen-month fight for survival and eventual rescue.

James Clavell's bestselling novel, 'King Rat' told a not so warming tale of sickness, starvation and even some actual gangrene, that was inflicted upon a motley crew of soldiers; fighting to survive the rigors of a Japanese POW camp during the second world war.

Even these unwelcome tales helped to fend off the worry and unease that we both felt.

Laying perfectly still through all those days and nights, while still trying to maintain composure, as the snow piled up all around us was completely and utterly mind destroying.

Fortunately for us, day four broke with much less wind and only intermittent squalls of snow. Aching to get some movement back into our withering frames, we ambled up the short rope to the ledge system above us. This was the exact same point that Steve had reached with Mugs all those years earlier.

Staying well away from the wall above the pillar, we peered upwards through swathes of mist and bore witness to unsettling volleys of rockfall crashing down around us from much higher up the face. We sat on our respective rocks feeling painfully downhearted, but both of us knowing full well that even if the weather cleared completely, it would be gravely dangerous to spend any amount of time in the direct line of fire.

Realizing that it would be pure suicide to continue, we made the call to bail.

Rappelling nine hundred feet while each of us straddling an oversized haulbag in almost white out conditions was nerve rattling, but as we neared the bottom, the sun peeked out again and soon we were touching down onto the glacier and floundering through deep, fresh snow over to our boulder to regain our skis. Brushing off the rock we sat and gazed up at the snow plastered pillar that had been home during our weeklong adventure. We both voiced the fact that we were very relieved to be done with it. Right then, as if to seal the deal, a massive avalanche came roaring down the face, just beyond the pillar. We watched uneasily as a million tons of snow came free falling down the rocky face, to land with a deafening whump not far from where we were sitting. With nerves freshly rattled we roped up and set off back to our base camp.

This was much easier said than done, for our distant dome tent only revealed itself for a moment before the clouds rolled in and turned the world back into a featureless, grey soup again. Luckily, Steve had managed to take a quick compass bearing of the camp and so we adopted a new strategy.

He would shout out directions to me as I carefully skied ahead of him while still maintaining visual contact in the swirling fog.

"Left a bit, right a bit, ok good."

I would stop when the compass bearing was pointing directly at me, then take in the slack rope. Steve would catch up and we would repeat the process all over again. This ruse seemed to work quite well until after about half a mile, the mists cleared for a moment and dead ahead of us loomed a huge rock wall guarded by a jumble of gaping crevasses. Our system was a complete failure for I had somehow managed to get us completely turned around. Thankfully, the mists parted for one more glimpse and we spied our tent; much nearer now and just down the way. We made it back without further incident and broke open some much-needed scotch.

The pair of us were far too weary to attempt our escape anytime soon, so we spent a couple of eerie but calming days lingering around camp, observing a continuous stream of tumbling avalanche snow clouds or the bullet loud cracks of distant rockfall emanating from all around us. Although happy to be situated safely out in the middle of the Ruth, there was the nagging dread that sooner or later we would have to ferry 500 pounds of equipment, three miles up a steepening glacier, to the Ruth Amphitheater pick-up point.

The snow around camp had turned into mush and we were sinking up to our genitalia every time we left the well-traveled trails. No plane could ever land in these conditions and so we had no choice. The anticipation of embracing a safe and comfortable outside world again spurred us into action, as we broke camp and loaded everything onto two sleds. Next, we attached tethers from the sleds to our harnesses, then donned skis and tied into a short climbing rope between us and began trudging up the glacier.

Towing these beasts was brutal; thigh busting, sweat soaking work.

As the snow and ice steepened and crevasses grew larger and more menacing, route finding became an issue and at one point, I watched and yelled with horror as Steve's sled began to slither sideways behind him, down into the icy depths of a nearby crevasse. Luckily, he quickly changed course and caught it in time. Soon we arrived at the pickup point; an area of hard snowpack, about the size of three or four playing fields.

A couple of aircraft were parked in the back and a handful of mostly female tourists were posing for group photos. It must have seemed like we took a wrong turn at the Arctic Circle, because they greeted us eagerly and quizzed us all about our recent goings on.

More than happy to oblige, we offered up some of the choicest tidbits.

It felt so pleasant to be around women and listen to the sound of amiable and sensual laughter again.

An hour later and right on time, our ski plane circled in and landed near us.

Once fully loaded, she labored to gain height again, but upon doing so, the pilot leveled out then asked us if we would like to fly by the South face of Dickey. After swooping through an alarmingly narrow cleft in the ridge, the whole south face opened up in full view, on the left side of the cockpit. It was a giant of a mountain. Our dark pillar looked so miniscule, way down below when compared to the rest of the wall.

Soon we were flying over our old basecamp and off to the land of real greenery.

Noel and Lynne were waiting for us when we touched down on the Talkeetna airfield. Jimmy had already departed to pursue pressing work commitments elsewhere.

After plenty of whoops, hugs, and high fives, we moseyed over to the Fairview Inn, where Noel, Steve and I feverishly recounted the worst of our mutual near misses.

Steve mockingly put the whole debacle down to all of us suffering from an attack of Snail eye. When pressed for details, he informed us that a snail retracts its eyes just before retreating into its shell. It was a Yosemite term which basically meant, to chicken out.

A little later, Noel, being an expert and avid fisherman determined that we all should seek urgent fishing therapy to alleviate any lingering, traumatic memories of the Ruth. The following morning, Steve, Noel, and I laid down enough cash to procure big rubber waders, sturdy fishing rods, lures and a high-speed jet boat to shoot us up the Talkeetna River at very high speed to a preferred fishing spot.

This was just what we needed. A warm, sunny beach overlooking a rushing, crystal clear river surrounded by nothing but pristine wilderness. The half dozen or so fisherman sharing our piece of heaven were reeling in colossal King Salmon with monotonous regularity, so I eagerly dressed the part; set my hook and waded into thigh deep water. Now these days I'm not very a patient fisherman and so after a couple of hours of not so much as a twitch of the rod, I was starting to get thoroughly pissed off.

As lunchtime rolled around and the day grew oppressively warmer, all the other fishermen (and Steve), were now lounging on the beach in small groups and knocking back cold ones. Hell bent on hooking absolutely anything, I stood my ground, casting my lure across the turbulent river and slowly reeling it back in. Suddenly I heard a loud splash coming from behind me. I looked back in shocked amazement, to find a very large silvery, speckled King salmon floating idly by in the shallows. In a flash, I hurled my rod onto the beach and plucked her out of the water. The poor girl still had a hook in her mouth and must have put up one hell of a fight further upstream. I ended her suffering and then weighed her. Forty pounds! I just couldn't believe my luck. Then I looked around and realized that nobody had even noticed my victorious catch. Soon Steve ambled back over, and I relayed my fishing tale to him. He suggested that we play a trick on Noel, who was engrossed in my same predicament, further down the beach.

"Hey Noel! Look what Strappo caught," yelled Steve.

Noel came racing towards us, as fast as his bibbed rubber waders would allow. We bit our tongues to try to maintain a straight face.

I easily discerned a face green with envy.

"Wow, Strappo. That's amazing. What kind of lure did you use?"

"Oh, the little pink and green one."

"Wow, OK. Where in the river did you hook it?"

"Do you see that little bit of smooth, green water in the middle? Right there."

Poor Noel spent the rest of the afternoon flinging lures into that bit of green water, but with no luck whatsoever. It wasn't until we returned all our rented fishing gear back to the store and started dinner back at the van, that Steve and I finally spilled the beans.

Noel feigned a look of being extremely hurt.

The following day was June 21st, the Summer Solstice. We'd heard tell of a big shindig out at the airfield for the locals, with live music and lots of beer.

I offered up my prize catch to the barbie and was proud to have her feed a long line of townsfolk and tourists alike.

Our grand finale before hitting the long road home was a flight to end all flights. It was Lynne's birthday and so we all chipped in and arranged a scenic flight for the three of us into the Kitchatna Spires, a remote and largely unexplored chunk of the Alaska range.

There were more unclimbed, big mountain walls here than I could ever imagine. I suddenly longed to be back among them again, risking life and limb for a chance to embrace their ethereal magnificence and then maybe just maybe, climb to the top of one.

First Pakistan and now Alaska. My aspirations to score big in the realm of expedition climbing were not quite living up to my expectations. After mulling over recent events back at my home in Boulder, I concluded that there would always be unforeseen realities at play. We had wilted at the prospect of surviving many days of starvation on Ladyfinger and more recently, the prospect of getting killed by a constant stream of rockfall on Mount Dickey. These were the kind of unplanned events that never surfaced during the wildly optimistic, initial planning stages of trips like these.

Oblivious to these harsh realities, I embarked upon yet more near catastrophic failures during the next couple of South American summers.

The gang upon arrival.

Committed. The Dark Pillar is in the background, right of the plane.

Preparing to sled the gear up to the Ruth Amphitheater

Basecamp from high on Mt. Dickey.

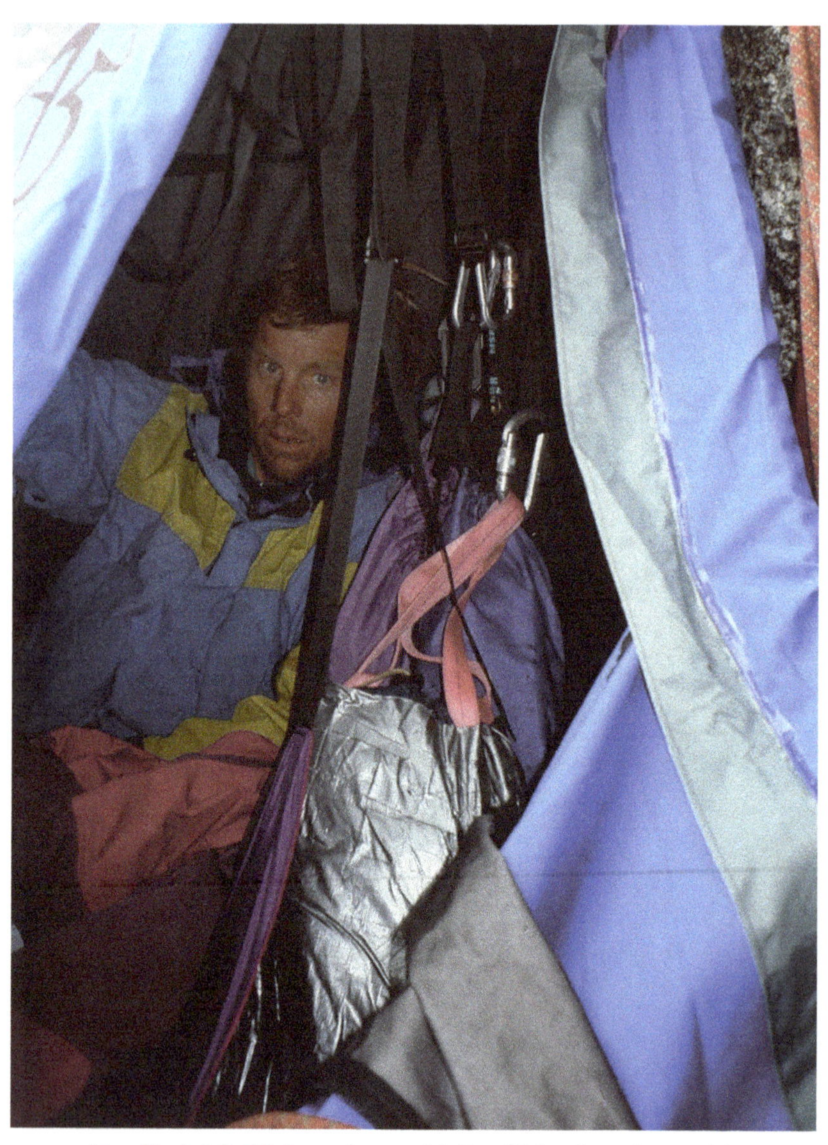

Go climb Mt Dickey, they said. It will be fun, they said!

Escaping after being pinned down for four days in a blizzard.

Catch of the day

Chapter 11. Jinxed Beyond Reason

"Only those that dare to fail greatly can ever achieve greatly."
  ~Robert F. Kennedy~

The patrons of Juanita's Bar were a veritable mine of useful information.

"So, what Spanish phrases should I learn for my upcoming trip to Patagonia?" I naively asked of my Latino friends, to the sound of much snickering and giggling.

After flying from Denver into Buenos Aires two weeks later, I spent that fateful morning staring at the airport's DEPARTURE board and completely missed the ARRIVAL of five British climbers, en route to attempt the giant (then) unclimbed East Face of Cerro Torre. Consequently, my epic solo 1700-mile overland trek to Patagonia was enlivened with the phrases.

"Five tequilas please," and "Look out! There are Llamas." I missed and/or paid too much for planes, buses, taxis, hotels, and meals and generally had an arduous and sucky time. With more bags of climbing hardware than I could physically carry, it was nothing shy of a miracle that I still managed to beat the team to base camp by four days.

Completely mystified and with zero knowledge of their whereabouts I played the waiting game, but boredom soon prevailed and one idle day I found myself rooting around the eerie and long abandoned: Cesare Maestri hut.

Nestled right on the edge of tree line, this ramshackle and brooding relic of the pioneering days was off limits as a nighttime shelter. Still. There could be no finer place to bask in total solitude while studying the colon-clinching, bayonet profile of Cerro Torre, poised high above the jumbled, chaotic glaciers.

In classic haunted house style, the door creaked melodiously open, and a newly disturbed sea of dust mingled with shafts of amber sunlight that emanated from chinks in the ancient timbers. Remnants of an old pot-bellied stove and a broken table lay strewn about. A few faded inscriptions caught my attention, but not much else.

That is until I happened to gaze up beyond the rafters.

There, tucked snugly away from prying eyes was a small metal crucifix. Overcome by temptation, I committed a stupid and sacrilegious error that might later return to haunt me,

Things started to go steadily downhill shortly after the team finally stumbled into camp.

We made it on to the face and fixed ropes up about six hundred feet of the smooth uncompromising wall, while glancing nervously at the enormous summit ice-mushroom overhanging our route far above. A five-man snow cave was excavated in the snowfield under the face. It too, was in the same line of fire.

As the weather turned a darker shade of nasty, we dumped a huge pile of big wall gear in the cave and marked the entrance with a bamboo wand, before retreating in the teeth of a savage, high-speed storm.

The weather raged on without respite for five, pitifully long weeks. We tried desperately to make it back to our cave, only to be beaten back every single time. In the end, we succeeded, and stripped our ropes from the face before spending a whole afternoon trying to locate the mouth of the cave. Only two inches of the wand were still visible, and we barely salvaged our equipment and headed for home.

I departed Patagonia with the taste of bile in my mouth and vowed never to return.

A man is only as good as his word however, for when the phone rang and fellow Englishman, Noel Craine offered me a place in his team the following year, I found myself drooling pathetically at the idea of going back.

This time the venue would be the Central Tower of Paine in neighboring Chile.

"You've gotta believe me Strappo. The weather is so-oo much better than where you were on Cerro Torre." Noel did have evidence of this sweeping climatic generalization, with his ascent of a dramatic multi-day aid line over on the East side of the Central Tower.

Our third member would be Simon Nadin, a bold York-shireman with a reputation for having a no fuss, quietly get things done approach.

I bowed to the inevitable and departed Colorado's crisp winter landscape to embark upon yet another deranged trek southwards.

This time I was greeted at the airport by Jorge, a great Chilean friend who had recently wintered in Telluride. Jorge loved to race cars.

We burned rubber across Santiago in time to catch up with another climber bound for Patagonia; Donna Raupp. Donna had waited patiently for us at the Bus Station. Based in Flagstaff, Arizona, she was on her way to Patagonia to meet the rest of her Anglo-American Women's team. They too would be attempting the Central Tower.

The two of us would travel together on the long journey towards the mountain. Aside from being a very competent climber, she was also fluent in Spanish, a huge relief to me after my previous travel fiasco.

Toasting the New Year by passing a bottle of Glenfiddich single malt whiskey to the guy next door can be quite a challenge, especially if like you, he also happened to be driving at over a 100 mph out of Santiago in the hope of catching a New Year's firework display at one of the oldest horse ranches on the American continent.

With a sickening lurch, Jorge punched both gas and gear-shift, sending the BMW careening across the highway, through the ranch entrance and into a nearby field, in a finely executed four-wheel drift. We came to an abrupt sideways halt just as the first fusillades of rockets erupted and the cheers of a delirious crowd drowned the night.

"Happy New Year. We made it, screamed an exuberant Jorge over the deafening explosions. I removed my clawed fingers from the upholstery and exhaled.

"Are we there yet?" yawned a plaintive voice from the back seat. In a very impressive display of nerve, Donna had slept through the entire ordeal, but upon casting her eyes at the crowds of poolside revelers, leapt out of the car, sprinted across the field, and threw herself into the mayhem.

As the party picked up, we experienced a true taste of fine Chilean hospitality and raged well into the night with these masters of the equestrian and all that is horsey.

Our hosts were very reluctant to let us leave and plied us with yet more fine food, wine, and beer,

With a bus to catch though, Donna and I bid fond and sad farewells to Jorge and all his friends as we finally began the long journey south to Patagonia.

Swanning through South America in a maelstrom of high adventure, amid a vivid backdrop of serene, aquamarine lakes, giant volcanoes and dense bamboo jungles was an expedition unto itself but was still a far cry from the wind-battered Towers of Paine.

By the twelfth of January, Noel, Simon, and I, plus the women's team comprising Celia, Gerry, Donna, and Alison had somehow converged upon the blustery, windswept town of Puerto Natales and were snugly ensconced in the Café Crystal, blissfully reunited and deep in wine.

The following day turned into the shop-a-thon from hell, but the net result was 1100 pounds of food and gear to be meticulously sorted, resorted then weighed into horse loads. By seven o'clock that evening, we were done and could finally contemplate the next morning's stampede up to base camp in the Torres Del Paine National Park.

Later that night, in the Malden Disco, we emulated a giant black hole and proceeded to devour all available wine and beer. Excitement reached a frenzied pitch, with a style of dancing that bore no resemblance to the rhythmic and sensual salsa dancing performed by the local townsfolk.

A nagging grey dawn eventually sent us stumbling back to the hostel, to barge into our respective rooms, to careen off walls, crash into bunk beds and then to sit, stand on and generally annoy the peacefully sleeping inhabitants.

The call to arms came only ninety minutes later.

"Come on you worthless sacks. The bus is outside. You have three minutes."

And so it came to pass that the expedition, burdened with blinding headaches, brewery breath and glazed, sunken eyes, first beheld the Towers of Paine from afar. The bus ride was unlike any other. "I think I'm going to be sick, whinnied Alison. A mutinous Celia was busy facing off against an angry mob of fare paying passengers as she discarded their soothing, familiar Pink Floyd tape in favor of our own rumpy pumpy dance tunes. I stared vacantly ahead, wishing only to die in peace, but suddenly a yell from the crowd had everyone clamoring for a first glimpse at the towers: three golden monoliths, a dusting of clean ice adorning each summit and behind them a sheer backdrop of unfathomable whiteness.

As the afternoon dragged merrily along, many insurmountable obstacles toppled and fell by the wayside. Passports, permits, and rescue insurance were all in order, so another short bus ride whisked us away from the park entrance and reunited us with our mountainous gear pile. Next to the gear sat a disgruntled and surly head Gaucho, who steadfastly refused to transport any gear up to base camp until morning. Too risky on the horses he said. We glumly moped around as torrential afternoon rain started to pelt us, then a horse bolted, and the Gauchos galloped off in hot pursuit. We all cursed in unison then scurried to a nearby hostel for shelter, some vile instant coffee, and a little damage assessment. Ashen-faced, I snook into one of the bedrooms for a little shuteye, but soon got busted. Five sleep-filled minutes later and the proprietor loomed over me, her eyebrow raised in a way that said, "Why don't you just go out and play?" I slunk meekly away to the equipment stash, grabbed a haul bag and commenced slogging.

Base camp was far more than idyllic. Aromatic, dew-soaked greenery blanketed the forest floor beneath bearded, grey lichens drooping from gnarled and twisted boughs. Heavy scented wood smoke lingered above a cabin lively with laughter and the chatter of climbers.

We soon adapted to a life of forest dwelling, but always with a watchful eye on the heavens. With hourly pre-dawn alarm calls throughout the night, the merest glimpse of a few stars had us stampeding out of the trees, along windswept moraines and up the enormous hourglass couloir that accessed the Central Tower. Tormented, we writhed with uncertainty as brutal storm systems ambushed one moment and then enticed with momentary clear blue skies the next. After many of these disheartening skirmishes, we threw a foot in the door by hiding a small tent behind snowdrifts at the base of the hourglass couloir.

As numbing whirlwinds of flying snow died momentarily, we settled into a review of the West face. Simon, Noel, and I instantly agreed on our goal, a superb unclimbed crack system that branched out from an existing line in the main, central corners.

The following day we hauled the fattest of loads up the couloir to the wall. This time the weather demons were elsewhere, and we grappled with the initial icy corners to a two-pitch high point. Happy to have made it onto the face, we fixed ropes and rappelled down, then butt-slid fiendishly sticky snow to regain our tent in time for a midnight cookout and insanely optimistic talk of nude summit photos.

The rest of this night was a rough one though, for the meatiest of chest infections had invaded my bronchials and I wallpapered the adjacent snowbank in thick, green phlegm. Broken sleep was cut bitingly short by Simon's 5.30am alarm call. Outside the palest hints of a salmon sunrise suggested another workable day. The soup chalice made its rounds before Simon and Noel set off towards the route, leaving me to wallow in abject misery. Sleep had long since departed, so I packed a day bag, dropped the tent and wobbled back down to friendlier surroundings and very hard drugs. An ecstatic Noel woke me around dinnertime and proudly announced that we now had ropes fixed up to the thousand-foot mark. I bolted out of bed wide eyed and pressed for details. Noel babbled on about sustained, often icy but near perfect cracks. "A few more pitches would bring us to a possible crossover into the unclimbed dihedrals. One long climbing day should see us on the summit," beamed Simon.

"Happy, happy, joy, joy," I wheezed, then slumped back on my bed, delirious with thoughts of our impending success.

My cold germs were gutless; they displayed little or no moral fiber and three days later, I was cured.

In the face of relentless foul weather, our strategies changed, and we transplanted our camp 3000' higher up the couloir and nestled our tiny bivi tent on a narrow, exposed ledge below the nearby North Tower. Perched so far above the icecap, we gazed in wonder as a chaotic landscape of snow swept summits, immense glaciers and speeding Technicolor cloud walls unfolded before us. A familiar predawn weather check: "Eee-vull." pronounced Noel, so it was happily back to bed, but soon after; we caught the unmistakable sound of approaching voices.

"Get out of bed you pansies, it's great out here." I exposed my face to a mildly hideous day and two big smiles.

Sean and Guy; two Canadian climbers, were on their way up to tackle the Monzino route over on the North Tower and stopped by to hassle us. We sprinted to the base of our route and got to work, jumaring heavily iced ropes up to the start of fresh terrain.

Inside the haul bag, our rack of hardware had somehow metamorphosed into a solid clump of ice but was soundly thrashed into submission before I set off on my pitch. Blade pins were pounded into icy seams as I warmed to the rhythm of steady aid climbing. In the worsening weather, I caught the faint howls as Sean and Guy summited the North Tower. A little jealous, I finished my pitch with a craving for fast and fluid alpine climbing. Simon cleaned the pitch as Noel jumared past me to take the lead. We were now just twenty feet away from accessing the line of corners that wended their way towards the summit, but a freight train wind thundered through the nearby Col Breche. Heavy snowfall soon turned the face into a spindrift nightmare, and so thwarted, we bailed down the fixed lines. The hour-glass couloir had already started flowing, so we merged with it and abandoned our high camp to the weather demons.

Terrible, terrible stuff. The storms raged on for ten straight days and Noel's pristine tent soon became torn to shreds. We salvaged the remains and fled in the face of a real heavyweight. This one dumped deep, wet snow below tree line and sent the entire camp into enforced hibernation. Bored and tent bound, sleep became a merciful escape from the cold and squalor of cabin life until one morning, I experienced a very close call indeed.

It was almost breakfast time, but this one particular dream could not be cut short. A float plane banked steeply above a cobalt ocean and far below, unknown friends waved at me from the shores of a sun-bleached coral island. Suddenly, an enormous weight slammed into the tent with immense force and sent me tumbling frantically towards the door.

I emerged into the blizzard to discover that a telegraph-sized tree branch had sheared from the weight of snow and had dropped fifty feet, to cleanly crush the tent just inches from where my feet lay. The small crowd of bewildered onlookers seemed vaguely surprised to see me alive. A huge grin from Noel. "You'd better think about returning that crucifix you stole before something really serious happens.

Of course, Noel was referring to the small iron crucifix that I had found high in the rafters of the Cesare Maestri hut three years earlier. It now adorned my bedroom wall back home.

I had felt quite guilty about taking it and had often talked about returning it someday.

Perhaps that someday should come sooner than later, for without the slightest tangible reason, our cabin burned to the ground two days later.

Yet another nightmarish drama ensued. In my subconscious, distant shouts from Noel in the dead of night. "Everybody wake up. Wake up, NOW!" An ominous glow filtered through the tent walls, but my fogged brain dismissed any kind of sunrise. Outside, the crackle of exploding timbers mingled with a terrifying and unmistakable roar as flames towered high above the treetops, fanned by a devil wind. The entire forest seemed likely to catch and the whole camp, shocked to the core, stood by helplessly.

Then the fuel cache caught fire.

Cases of propane cylinders and liters of white gas exploded like starburst incendiaries, flinging blazing shrapnel into the night. We formed a human chain from the river and fought the fire using a pathetic array of buckets and pans. Mercifully, the forest was still soaked from the recent rains and by sunrise we had the fire contained. Coughing hard and thoroughly blackened, we retired to our respective tents for a one-hour power nap before starting the big clean up.

Homeless and practically foodless, the exodus began in earnest as a slew of climbers bailed back to the civilized world to resupply and plan for a possible comeback.

Those climbers with more than half a functioning brain cell caught the early flights out, to pursue happier lives elsewhere, while Noel, Simon and I promptly extended our tickets and tempted the gods with another expensive tent by setting up home back at the base of the Hourglass couloir once again.

Dogged by empty, frustrating days, we were finally rewarded with a snippet of indifferent weather. Noel and Simon risked another journey back up the fixed ropes as the wind slowly relented and the clouds parted. I spent the day rebuilding our next base camp cabin, while also writhing with weather uncertainties.

Later in the day, my intrepid cohorts made the transfer into virgin territory and grappled with ever steepening corners; blank in the back, but luckily sporting a thin hand crack that split the left wall, allowing for some outrageous 5.11 stemming on impeccable granite. Down in the forest, the first stars arrived early in the palest of evening skies. The dying sun's rays stained the surrounding hillsides in a rich ochre. Weather doubts vanished, and with the housing project completed, I sped my way across the bleak moraines and up the couloir to intercept Noel and Simon at the base of the route at about one in the morning. In an inky blackness, we unearthed the haul bag from beneath four feet of fresh snow and dug in for the night. This turned out to be a well-intentioned but dimwitted maneuver, as we spent a bitter night huddled inside a flysheet without sleeping bags or pads, hoping, praying for just one more fine day.

On week number ten in the land of the devil storm; our wish was very nearly fulfilled.

On a fiercely cold but stable day in mid-February we succeeded in climbing the wall, and in doing so were privileged to experience the very best that Patagonia had to offer. Technically demanding but also friendly and well protected pitches. These magnificent cracks eventually landed us at a series of ledges that offered a once in a lifetime panorama, perched far above the surrounding peaks.

As darkness gently fell, a distant shout from Simon had Noel and I both frantically simul-climbing over a cavernous 'A-frame' roof that, we knew from our surveillance, signified the very last of the difficulties. Unexpected problems then arose. Beyond the belay lay a few hundred feet of loose and completely featureless slabs, and in the gathering gloom we chose a line that sent us far into a cul-de-sac. Breathless and tired, we reunited back at the belay and considered our options. An ugly cloud base rose from the valleys below and was compounded by the uncertainty of route finding at night. This allowed the worst kind of agony to set in. Above, a summit that looked close enough to touch, and below us, another impending storm. The 2000' of fixed rope beckoned. We hit the fixed ropes with little doubt that the summit was now firmly in the bag.

Another week drifted by, and with it came yet another mission to resupply in Puerto Natales. It was early morning. I lay there, wide awake in my bunk after a curiously sleepless night. The hostel's proprietor stood in the doorway calling my name: a telephone call from the British Consul. My sister had just been savagely murdered; stabbed to death in a senseless robbery in our hometown of Liverpool. As I boarded the first of many buses and planes toward the rest of my family, I suddenly found myself unable to express a simple request, but amid all the tearful hugs and goodbyes; it finally came out.

"For God sakes, please summit this damn mountain, for all of us and all that we've been through together."

Ten days later, Noel and Simon journeyed back up the fixed ropes towards the summit of the Central Tower of Paine. Ironically, one of the ropes, less than three weeks old, had snapped in the wind, separating them from an easy summit victory. Unable to proceed, they stripped the wall and continued their expedition to other, more hospitable areas. Every ounce of climbing gear that I owned sat at the top of that wall, waiting to be claimed by another, luckier climbing team.

Laden with grief and tears, I returned to my home country to console and protect my mother from a continuous stream of enquiring well-wishers.

After the funeral I made a solemn vow to the return the crucifix to its exact original location.

It's back there now so if you ever come across it, my advice is…please; leave it be.

Cerro Torre

Torres del Paine

Surviving the fifty-foot branch falling onto the tent.

Leigh and his snuggle buddy outside the bar in El Chalten.

Chapter 12 Beaches, Boats, and Barstools

"Obstacles are those frightful things you see when you take your eyes off the goal."
~Henry Ford~

I'd recently heard vague rumors of the party to end all parties, straight from the horse's mouth.

The 'Baja Ha-Ha' was a two-week sailboat regatta that ran from San Diego, California to Cabo San Lucas on the southern tip of Mexico's Baja peninsula. The horse's mouth belonged to one my greatest friends, Steve Morris. He was a seasoned alpinist and a damn good rock climber, but more importantly, he was also a supremely competent Alaskan offshore fishing captain.

The notion of joining a flotilla of swanky, ocean-going yachts, jam packed with bikini clad beauties for a two weeklong party had me instantly foaming at the mouth with acute longing.

Steve and I had first met back in Yosemite's Mountain Room Bar during that period of evening insanity seventeen years earlier. He was a very dependable guy and always followed through with his goals. I relished spending time with him out on the open ocean or carousing the raucous evening beach parties that would soon become our nightly fare.

Then one evening the phone rang. It was Steve. He informed me that the fishing season was about to kick off earlier than expected and that he had to cancel on the Baja Ha-Ha. I was completely gutted, and I think Steve could sense my abject disappointment because a little later in the conversation he suggested that I get in touch with another skipper buddy of his; Chris Beehan. I called him up as soon as we hung up and a gruff but enthusiastic voice answered. Chris, it seemed, lived in Montauk, Long Island in southeastern New York State. Chris talked of his upcoming plan to sail his seventy-foot aluminum racing sloop called Cinnabar from Montauk out to the island of Bermuda and then head south, all the way down to Trinidad to give Cinnabar an affordable refit. It didn't seem to faze him when I mentioned that I had zero sailing experience. He'd already enlisted his friend Larry from New Jersey and would be happy to have me aboard as a third helping hand.

And so, it was agreed. I would meet Chris at the boat in less than two weeks' time and I would spend the following months learning to sail offshore in the farthest, most remote reaches of the Atlantic Ocean.

Then, out of the blue, fate stepped in with an unprecedented turn of events.

Tim Waring worked at the Telluride mountaineer, a climbing store down on main street in Telluride, Colorado.

One afternoon, while chatting amicably with a small group of my good friends in the store, he learned about my forthcoming sailing trip and called me up later that day.

"Hello, Strappo. You don't know me. My name is Tim. I heard that you were planning to sail down to Trinidad. How would you like to go climbing with me in the jungles of Venezuela afterwards?"

Tim went on to reveal that the year before, he had taken a scenic flight out beyond Angel Falls and had discovered immense, unclimbed big walls, perhaps thousands of feet high. He also went on to inform me that he had work commitments at the climbing store up until just before Christmas but would be free after that.

"Hell, yeah Tim, that sounds amazing," I replied. "If I'm still down there, I'll meet you in Caracas airport one week before Christmas, and I'll wear a ridiculous Beavis and Butthead T-shirt, so you'll recognize me in the crowd."

And so, it was settled. I would stash all my big wall climbing gear on the boat and sail southwards with an unknown skipper then hop into Venezuela and try to learn Spanish while waiting for my unknown climbing partner to arrive!

"This was going to be one hell of an adventure," I mused.

Then it occurred to me that this might just be the kick in the ass that I needed, the ultimate venue for my next climbing expedition.

I started tallying up my previous mountaineering track record. It was certainly nothing to write home about. In the last eight years, I had narrowly failed to reach the summit on seven mountain big walls. I let the list run painfully through my head.

Two in Patagonia.

Cerro Torre and the Central Tower of Paine. (weather), (unforeseen circumstances).

Three more in Alaska.

The South Face of Mount Dickey (fear)

An unnamed sea cliff 40 miles south of Juneau. (weather)

One more in Punchbowl Cove in the Misty Fiords National Monument. (weather).

One in Northern Canada. Lotus Flower Tower. (weather)

And finally, one in Pakistan. Biblimotin- aka Ladyfinger. (starvation)

Bad climber! Bad, bad climber!!

Depression began to overwhelm me. All that scrimping and saving; all the failed relationships and sacrifices that I'd made in the name of being such an obstinate and obsessively driven climber.

The shame of defeat and self-doubt festered from deep within. Perhaps I would quit this bullshit game altogether and set my sights on more attainable goals.

But was the universe trying to tell me something? Could this really be my big break?

If the only obstacle standing between me and a virgin summit in Venezuela was merely a few jungle shrubberies, then why not give it my very best shot. Jungle climbing could really be the one, and this time there would be NO backing down.

Suddenly, I was ready to take on the world again.

Time crawled by painfully until finally the day came when I was staring blankly out of the window of Montauk's Liar's Saloon at one beautiful, signal green, single masted, all aluminum racing sloop, moored to the rickety wooden dock, not more than fifty yards away.

While he appeared rather large and a little imposing, I could already tell that Chris would be a patient, good-natured skipper. After several beers we were joined by Larry. He carried a strong Jersey accent and I soon warmed up to this off beat character and his almost pant wetting sense of humor.

Chris informed us that the Cinnabar had served her time as a naval training vessel. He had recently purchased her and was keen to remodel her exactly to his liking. Unfortunately, shipwright work in the New York area was ruthlessly expensive and so we were to sail in search of an affordable contractor at our final destination; Port-of-Spain on the Caribbean Island of Trinidad. I was well psyched, for the island was only a stone's throw from the pristine equatorial beaches of northern Venezuela.

The following morning, we loaded up the Cinnabar with gear and supplies while waiting for the tide to rise and so facilitate our departure. I was feeling a little pensive; highly aware that we were heading out into the North Atlantic at the height of hurricane season, where the normally 3–4-foot ocean swells could suddenly rear up and get a whole lot higher and more dangerous.

Soon we were weaving our way out of the harbor and hoisting the twin sails under a steady breeze. The Cinnabar picked up speed, with her bow aimed at a faint line marking a point where the ocean ended, and the sky began. The coastline gradually disappeared from view and quite soon we were completely alone, with nothing around us but a brooding, gunmetal ocean.

As we settled into a life at sea, Chris gave Larry and I a few pointers on various winches and the specific drill for raising and lowering the sails. Our skipper did most of the work however and with the vessel usually set on autopilot, our main tasks were keeping watch while the other two crew members slumbered. I took the midnight to 4am and noon to 4pm watches. An unbreakable rule was to always remain clipped into an anchor point with a running leash while at the wheel. My nighttime vigils were usually a fight to stay awake and maintain vigilance, but with zero artificial light, it was a perfect time to revel in the milky way, ablaze with billions of stars, all to the soothing rhythm of waves trilling against Cinnabar's metallic bow. On my second night on watch I was suddenly startled by the appearance of two dazzling meteors falling from the heavens and aiming towards our destination: Bermuda. They hung in the night sky for almost a full minute before fading from view.

Soon we had to enter the choppy, sixty-mile-wide Gulf Stream, which originates in the Gulf of Mexico then flows through the Florida Strait and up the east coast before breaking off into the north Atlantic and beyond. This unpredictable stretch of ocean required careful scrutiny of all weather predictions and was a place that demanded a level of respect; with a warm current moving at a steady four miles per hour and with a distance to the ocean floor of nearly 4000 feet. The Gulf Stream was also a magnet for sudden, menacing storms.

Cinnabar took the prevailing conditions well in her stride, with the sails bowed down under a ripping wind; she reached a record top speed for the voyage, scraping in at 28 knots.

The level of solitude was far beyond anything I'd ever experienced before. I relished not seeing any sign of human existence for days on end. But halfway through my watch during the following night, distant lights suddenly appeared out on the horizon.

I watched intently as the lights slowly grew in size as the ship approached. From below decks came the peaceful snoring of my crew mates.

Hating to disturb them, I hoped the ship would pass us by at a safe distance, but No. The fully loaded freighter bore down on us as if on a vindictive mission to sink us. Unbelievable! Not a soul in days and now this. "Chris! Wake up, I think we have a problem!"

Chris stumbled bleary eyed up on deck and quickly spun the wheel, causing Cinnabar to veer off to starboard and escape near disaster.

It was a slightly unsettling moment for me right then, for I suddenly realized that, had I dozed off for even a few short minutes we might all have died a violent, senseless death. I resolved to be a lot more careful in future.

Reeling in large, meaty oversized tuna didn't seem to be an issue. Chris impressed us once again with his cordon bleu prowess, but when I spied the bloody veins of the perfectly sushified fish, my stomach contents bade me farewell, with an urgent request to take a quick dive overboard.

We first clasped our eyes on the faint outline of Bermuda towards the end of my watch on night four, and then the encircling whiteness of crashing reefs. They extended as far as ten miles out from the north end of the island and so it took us the remainder of the night and part of the morning to carefully navigate around them.

Setting foot on land again felt good but a little wobbly. After a brief visit to the harbormasters office, we made tracks to the nearest British looking pub for a few morning liveners, which increased our rate of wobble by a factor of twelve.

A week on Bermuda was just enough time to get a real feel for the place, with its antiquated, laid-back island lifestyle and beautiful pink sand beaches.

I managed to really piss Chris off one morning with the sudden, mutual discovery of a missing flagpole with its five-foot stars and stripes flag from back on the stern. The previous evening's bad behavior filtered back to my pickled brain in dribs and drabs. The three of us had fallen in with a group of cruise ship stewardesses at the bar and as the evening dragged loudly on, Chris expressed a keenness to take the dinghy and motor back to the Cinnabar. Larry and I were far too busy leering drunkenly at these lovely ladies to pay him much attention, so when the bar closed, it came to our attention that we would have to swim in shark infested waters; weaving around many other anchored sailboats in the dead of night; half a mile back to the mother ship, if we could even find her.

Apparently, this was what we did, but upon our spluttering, cross-eyed, breast stroking arrival, latching onto the side of the boat was just not happening at first. After a few fruitless tries, I kicked my feet super hard and sprung from the water like a breaching whale; just catching the edge of the deck with my fingertips at full stretch.

The rest of the exit maneuver became a shameful and embarrassing confession the next morning.

Still reeking of booze and on the brink of death, I donned Chris's scuba gear and scoured the seabed for a long time in search of our American flag, but to no avail. It would be a couple of weeks later during our stay in St John in the Virgin Islands before I could borrow a wood shop, purchase some mahogany, and fabricate a new flagpole; thus, restoring Cinnabar to her former glory.

As our fun filled week on the island drew to a close, Larry hopped on a flight back to the mainland to resume his more normal life. Chris and I carefully restocked the boat with supplies sufficient for a couple of weeks.

After a careful weather check, we set sail on our next leg of the journey down to St John. Set sail might have been a bit optimistic though, for there was not a puff of wind on that hot, sultry morning. The engine purred rhythmically as we idled slowly out of the harbor and back out into the vast, open ocean. Venturing southwards, we narrowly skirted the northern tip of the infamous Bermuda Triangle.

Ever since my early childhood days, I had always been intrigued by this mysterious patch of alleged weirdness. Spanning as much as 1.5 million square miles, this vague triangle of ocean stretched from Puerto Rico in the south, over to the tip of Florida and on up to Bermuda. The US Navy estimated that as many as 50 ships and 20 aircraft had gone missing there. Myths and legends abounded, and conspiracy theorists have offered up many possible explanations, ranging from alien abductions to enormous bubbles of methane gas rising up from the ocean floor. Two of the biggest mysteries remain unsolved to this day.

Sometime after March 4th, 1918, the USS Cyclops disappeared without trace, along with a crew of 309 hands. It was the single largest loss of life in the history of the US Navy not related to enemy fire.

The second big, unsolved mystery involved Flight 19. This was a training flight with five American torpedo bombers that disappeared off radar on December 5th, 1945. A search and rescue aircraft deployed to look for them also disappeared without trace, along with it's 13-man crew.

This wasn't the kind of stuff to dwell on as we journeyed south without so much as a hint of a breeze on a sea of glass for the ensuing seven nerve-wracking days. In a desperate attempt to conserve precious fuel, we hoisted the three-sided spinnaker sail off the bow at the sight of even the merest puffy cloud in the hope of gaining some headway but all to no avail. We would soon learn that the reason for the dead calm conditions was in fact due to a major Category 5 hurricane. We were sailing on the flip side and luckily far from imminent danger; being more than a thousand miles away from Hurricane Mitch, the second deadliest Atlantic hurricane on record. As we motored south, Mitch was busy unleashing all her fury in Central America in a nightmare of horrific flooding and sustained 180 mph winds.

The final death toll would be an unthinkable 7000 people in Honduras and another 3800 in Nicaragua.

It struck home to me just how committing offshore sailing really was, being so at the complete mercy of all the elements, in a deadly serious 'luck of the draw' gamble.

But after seven frustrating but uneventful days we closed in on the Virgin Islands and the wind finally picked up. Then the faint suggestion of palm trees on the horizon sent a sudden rush of elation mixed with immeasurable relief. Soon, the darker ocean gave way to dazzling aquamarine coastal waters as we neared land and finally entered St John's harbor. We had made a safe landing with the fuel dipstick showing an almost empty tank.

I was overjoyed to make it this far down into the Caribbean, with the unknown skipper who turned out to be not only a highly competent seaman but also a true friend. I pondered on what the Venezuelan jungle would be like later on, and what kind of climbing partner mystery Tim would be. I still had six weeks to kill before meeting him in Caracas airport, resplendent in my highly visible Beavis and Butthead t-shirt, so I put all thoughts aside and focused on just living for the moment and having fun.

Chris, it seemed, knew many of the locals and I was introduced to many folks as the crazy climber en route to South America. During evenings in the pub, I made a great many good friends and quite soon I was offered a job, trimming out a small Patagonia retail store on the main street. My morning commute generally involved waking up with a moderate to severe hangover and rowing my rubber dinghy into shore, grabbing a quick coffee and bagel, and getting to work. It was a blessing to be exercising my withering muscles again while making some much needed cash. I was having a blast and St John really felt like home to me. I was in awe of just how laid back everybody was. One evening, I watched from a nearby balcony as a police patrol car drove up and two uniformed cops got out. They walked over to the bar and ordered a couple of bottles of Red Stripe lager, then got back in their cop car with said lagers and drove away! Apparently, there were no open container laws here and the legal drinking age was only eighteen. I hadn't seen much evidence of rampant alcoholism during my stay and couldn't help but wish that everywhere else on the planet might follow suit.

Wishful thinking on my part obviously.

As the weeks rolled by in my island paradise, I started to get a little antsy and started to feel a renewed urge to move on and continue my journey towards Venezuela.

I had met a non-English-speaking Venezuelan back in Boulder, Colorado earlier in the year. I had employed Oscar Gonzales and his buddy Carlos to help me with a big deck project. We'd had great times and a lot of laughs. It turned out that Oscar owned a night club in the mountain college town of Merida, high up in the Venezuelan Andes. Oscar also ran a tourist hostel high up above the town and so was keen to return my hospitality by offering me a place to stay while waiting for Tim to arrive before Christmas.

My itchy feet also happened to coincide with another turn of events.

Chris had recently met an attractive, fun-loving woman and they had started spending time together. Suddenly, Chris did not feel an urgent need to sail down to Trinidad to get started on Cinnabar's extensive remodel.

With the retail store completed I was now a free agent again and so it was decided.

After saying our fond farewells, I took a dawn ferry ride over to the neighboring island of St Thomas where I boarded a small aircraft bound for San Juan, Puerto Rico.

As we left the ground, I could barely take my eyes off an incredibly beautiful woman seated across from me and was far too spellbound to even mumble a hello to her.

The captain chimed in on the intercom upon takeoff and announced that we were traveling with the newly crowned Miss World! She was heading back to her home island of Trinidad.

I was already starting to regret jumping ship. Maybe I should have stuck it out, if the women down there were anywhere near as beautiful as her...

After my connecting flight touched down in Caracas airport, the merest hint of an epic began to unfurl when my enormous haul bag containing all the expedition gear failed to show up on the carousel. I was informed that my bag would probably show up in Merida in no later than three days' time. The next glitch in my travel plan came with the cancellation of my flight up into the Andes due to a low cloud ceiling. The nearest I could possibly get to Merida was a alternate flight to an obscure town on the flatlands and then a long taxi ride up there. I arrived later that evening feeling very travel weary and worn out. With only a vague name on Oscar's hand drawn map I implored the taxi driver to help me find the club. After carousing several dark streets in a torrential downpour, we located the dim, neon lights of the main entrance and I was soon engrossed in trying to convey who I was to the two intimidating bouncers in my very limited Spanish.

"Hola amigo, estoy un amigo de Oscar. ¿Donde el?"

Oscar was not at the club and so I was issued a flyer for his hostel (La Posada), up in the mountains. Another taxi was summoned, and we sped off into the night once again. After a lengthy drive up dark, windy roads and a little back tracking, my driver pulled onto the side of the road next to a vague track heading up into an even darker forest. There was a definite look of concern on his face.

"Tienes luz?" he repeated over and over again. I had no clue what he was saying until he gestured with an imaginary flashlight in his hand.

Of course, I did not. Practically everything that I owned was in the haul bag and God knows where that was. All I had with me was my carry-on day pack containing a few light clothes and a wash kit. I thanked the driver and set off into the forest; dressed only in jeans and a tank top, with a bath towel draped over my head. The rain was merciless as I groped my way blindly along the wooded trail, occasionally crawling on my hands and knees while praying not to lose the track and end up lost and alone in the forest.

The rain eased to a lighter drizzle and after a while I caught the faint outline of a steep, mountainous hillside to my left. I had exited the trees and now could discern the trail in front of me. As my eyes readjusted to the near total darkness, I began to make out various ramshackle houses above me, then one of them just happened to catch my attention. Outside the front door was a night light that lit up the word 'Posada.' Of more interest though was a large, spiral, open hand motif, which matched the one on Oscar's flyer.

"Oh my god, please let this be it!"

I beelined up the open hillside to the house and started nosing around on the veranda. All was dead quiet, and all the window shutters were closed, so out of complete and utter desperation I started thumping my fist on the front door, but no lights came on and nobody appeared in the doorway.

I tried the door, but it was locked.

There were other doors along the side of the house, and I tried one of them at random. This one was open, so I risked a peep inside. Bunk beds. Far beyond caring and without a second thought I collapsed on the nearest one and instantly fell asleep.

I awoke the next morning to the sound of footsteps outside the door. It was still dark in the room with the shutters closed and so there was no way of knowing if the owner of the footsteps was a friend or foe. I cracked the door and risked a glance in both directions. Nobody there. I tiptoed catlike down the veranda towards the front door and peeked around the corner with my heart in my mouth.

And there he was!

Oscar nearly jumped out of his skin when I called his name. Sudden shock gave way to a beaming smile as it dawned on him who was standing in front of him outside his house. None other than that crazy Brit from Boulder, Colorado, Estados Unidos!

My haul bag arrived at Merida's small airport as promised three days later.

Life soon resumed normally again. I caught the crowded transit van 'bus' down into Merida most mornings and had ample time to eat good food, take scenic hikes, meet cute girls but not understand them, go bouldering, and even take the cable car to the summit of the nearby Pico Bolivar, Venezuela's highest mountain. Evenings were spent back at the Posada getting to know various visiting tourists and drinking plenty of Polar, the country's favorite brand of lager. Life in Venezuela's countryside was tranquil and a very welcome break from all the high adventure that had brought me to this place.

Soon it was time to catch a plane back to Caracas and meet up with 'mystery' Tim and embark upon a second round of even crazier escapades.

The t-shirt recognition idea worked, and the mystery was no more.

Tim fought his way through the tightly packed airport crowd and introduced himself with a vigorous, spirited handshake as we fired a constant barrage of questions at each other. He was a little skinnier than me, but we were basically equal in stature and clearly, we shared the same passion for the upcoming adventure.

As we made our way towards the bus terminal, I pressed Tim for more details about what we were getting into down south. Tim rattled on about vast big walls of ancient Precambrian sandstone, long arduous jungle approaches, swollen rivers and waterfalls almost equal in size to Angel Falls, the world's largest uninterrupted waterfall. We would fly by bush plane into an indigenous Pemon Indian village, then hike across miles of open savannah, before beating trail through the jungle and up to the wall; where we would set up a base camp and begin our assault on the wall.

Just one hectic week after first meeting Tim in Caracas airport, the real adventure began in earnest.

Chapter 13. The Vulture's Garden

"I hope to arrive at my death late, in love and a little drunk."
  ~Atticus~

"Hey Tim. There's something hissing at me."

I had just deemed myself worthy; having hauled body and limbs free from the dank seeping corners after an all-out war with precarious blocks, oozing carpets of grass and thick, glutinous mud. These final moves had involved tunneling up through the soggy boughs of a decomposing tree to land at a small, unstable ledge some two hundred feet above a loud Venezuelan jungle. The big, red ants were out patrolling this tree, a solitary and highly aggressive kind that the Pemon people called 'Veinte Quattro's. They inflicted an excruciating sting that could last for twenty-four hours; a sting that I had recently savored and now took great lengths to avoid.

This newfound ledge also served as shower base as I squinted myopically through drenching curtains of water cascading down from rock ceilings higher up on the wall.

An ugly mess of dead tree roots clung meekly to the bulge directly above my head, but extensive yard work soon cleared the way for some delicate maneuvers to exit the waterfall and access much cleaner rock sweeping rightwards toward a short chimney and a potential hideaway haven.

Invigorated by the drenching, I launched into the traverse, with fingers blindly caressing the rippling, pale sandstone to reveal subtle finger pockets and sneaky, hidden side-pulls. Protection was sparse though and all I managed to place was a hastily slotted wired nut behind a dubious sounding flake. Fifteen feet beyond this wire and any composure I'd had was pummeled to oblivion, when a series of irreversible moves funneled me towards the final approach into the chimney. Only six more feet to go, but now I suddenly find myself staring at a fearfully blank rock surface as would a bug to a giant, ceramic tile. Dreamlike, I watched the me that fumbled these next moves go tumbling downwards and impact against the jagged side of the pillar far below. I shook the vision loose and tried to smear the edge of my outstretched climbing shoe into the middle of the tile. Without warning, the foot instantly skated, and fingertips flexed and strained even harder to maintain balance.

With waning strength and gulping breath I frantically pounded a blade piton into a hairline seam at eye level, only to hear it bottom out and become useless. Too terrified to even clip the piece, I clawed my way past it and struck the exact, same pose, then, with only fantasy friction, vaulted my entire body into the base of the shattered chimney and a future life.

Choking back pure adrenalin, I yelled down the complete blow by blow to a bored and despondent Tim as he mashed yet another Veinte Quattro to ant paste.

But the chimney was not a safe haven, for a giant, wedged boulder held in place by a walnut-sized pebble loomed overhead. With feet pressed firmly against both sides of the chimney, I dropped a shoulder and reached high with the other arm fully extended, inching my way past the death block until fingertips latched securely to the bottom edge of a wide, horizontal crevice. I matched hands and prepared to pull myself up into the slot when a loud hissing sound next to my head sent me howling back down the chimney.

"Tim. There's something hissing at me."

Now I really do admire snakes, but not enough to merit goading this one into biting me in the eye socket as I peeped nervously into the slot.

After much discursive yelling, it was agreed that I should place a solid anchor down inside the shady confines of the chimney and well out of reach from whatever lurks above.

I hauled up the bolt kit and began drilling my anchor in the steel-hard, Pre-Cambrian sandstone. The loud ringing of the hammer prompted another chilling noise from above, but this time in the form of a long, low Cujo snarl. Utterly mystified, I clipped the newly placed bolt, hoisted myself up and leaned back for a better view. I gagged on a sudden jolt of terror, for right there in front of my face squatted a very large vulture, his single malevolent eye glaring down from behind a razored stiletto beak. He emitted another growl and spread his wings at me, revealing a capacious wingspan, then in a flash, made a terrible beak-slashing strike towards my face, causing me to fall backwards. While sagging limply out of range, I contemplated being ripped to shreds by this demonic, flesh-tearing gargoyle. In a flurry of feathers, he would rip me wide open and then with a bemused look on his crooked head, gloat as I slowly bled to death.

I belayed Tim up the pitch. Blessed with the security of the rope, he joined me without too much difficulty. "Nice lead, well done."

"What should we do now?"

Luckily, today was our day to run completely out of food and so the call to flee was easily made. A call to run as far away from this inhospitable place as possible.

The preceding couple of weeks had really taken their toll on our nerves, with far too many close calls and near misses. At the outset, back at the start of this crazed adventure and on the night before our scheduled flight into the jungle, Tim had been mugged and severely beaten.

The drama had unfolded in our final outpost of urban existence, a bustling mining town called Santa Elena De Uiaren. Only through extreme good fortune and dogged perseverance had we managed to fly in and stage an assault on this hauntingly beautiful, cliff-edged mountain. To the indigenous Pemon people it is known as; 'Apauray Tepui', which literally means- The Coffin. We had just survived our first week alone, unarmed and in an unfamiliar jungle just teeming with unwelcome surprises.

After forging trails and establishing a base camp, we began the grueling task of trying to set foot on The Coffin itself. This had proved a major disappointment, for the climbing had turned out to be grossly unpleasant and not without it's many dangers. Yes, we were more than ready to beat an escape back to a more 'civilized' world.

A QUICK RECAP: Back to that ill-advised night out. In the town where it all began.

We had spent a tiring day stockpiling all the necessary food and equipment prior to our next morning's dawn flight to the Pemon village of Wonken.

With the last of the food boxes taped shut and hardware haul bags weighed, we embarked upon one final night of heavy drinking, starting with some foul screwcap wine with dinner.

Later, in a classic display of textbook stupidity, we ignored all the most basic rules of travel by first caning two bottles of rum and then stumbling into a disco in the shadiest part of town.

Much later and barely conscious, we somehow managed to get separated. A very bad move. Tim ended up in a dark alley with the wrong kind of people. Then came the clincher. He inadvertently pulled out a wallet just brimming with our hard cash. Two men took him down and proceeded to beat on him until the evil alley neighbors emerged to join in with some choice kicks about the head and chest. That next morning, a well damaged Tim was released from hospital, and I helped him hobble to the nearest bar for a thorough debriefing. Of course, we had both behaved like complete cretins, but were very relieved that no weapons had been used in the attack.

Fortunately for Tim, all his injuries; the ground rash and bleeding eyeballs, although hideous to look at, were only superficial. The immediate problem now concerned our dwindling cash supply, for the theft had left us so close to broke that a plane ride towards The Coffin would no longer be an option. So here we were, stuck in the southernmost point in Venezuela, only five miles away from the Brazilian border with barely enough cash to make it back to Colorado, USA.

Aimless, beer-swilling days drifted by. Tim made a rapid recovery but didn't get a whole lot prettier. His wounds did heal well enough to allow us to pursue other goals not requiring plane travel. We decided to embark upon another misguided adventure, but this time in the form of a minor hitch-hiking epic along the only paved road in this entire wilderness, armed with nothing more elaborate than a rough beer napkin sketch of some other, potentially unclimbed Tepuis.

As the fleet of flatbed semis rumbled northwards, a bleak, charcoal cloud ceiling stifled any possible glimpses of the famed jungle big walls. Two hours later, the trucks pulled into a bustling Indian village perched next to a wildly spectacular waterfall. We meekly inquired inside the nearest hut as to the possibility of climbing any nearby Tepuis, should they really exist. "Try asking the chief," came a polite and helpful reply. "He lives about eighteen kilometers in that direction, just past that clump of trees out on the horizon. Oh. Watch out for the river crossing on the way."

And so next morning, with crushing snake, biting fish, and losing our way paranoia, we set out across the savannah with truly monolithic pack loads. Luckily, the river crossing was only chest deep and soon afterwards the clouds lifted to reveal magnificent rock walls far off in the distance. "Just look at those things, they're sick!" marked Tim. We sucked breath as curling wisps of stratified cloud circled slowly around the distant Tepuis before melting away. "That approach looks way jungley though," I ventured, eyeing the thickset carpet of dense rainforest stretching for miles in every direction from out beyond the savannah.

We soon picked up a faint trail that skirted the many sections of jungle. These grasslands extended to the horizon at one point and the vastness of this region struck home when I came to realize that a huge, smokestack cloud rising up from where the earth disappeared was in reality a plume of mist rising from some gigantic waterfall, probably somewhere just inside British Guyana.

We sauntered blindly onwards as late afternoon squalls loomed and menaced, until, with more luck than common sense, we crested a hill and through steady sweeps of grey drizzle, spied a solitary thatched hut. A long-forsaken outpost and the first sign of human life that we'd seen all day.

The chief and his family greeted us at the threshold of the hut with beaming smiles and a large earthen bowl containing a viscous and lightly alcoholic beverage known as 'Kicheeri.' We enquired as to its origin. It seemed that a local root vegetable was ground to mush and later chewed into submission by toothless old crones. Fully hideous, but I marveled at its refreshing taste and began to ponder upon the idea of opening a Kicheeri brew pub back in Colorado, employing manic crews of master chewers.

I was very much in awe of my surroundings, for we appeared to be the first foreigners to visit with this family and became objects of great curiosity. After meeting Mom and a brethren of shy and giggling kids, Tim and chiefy got down to business. The man spoke very limited Spanish and so Tim tweaked his brain while attempting to communicate our plans. Twenty minutes of intense gibbering interspersed with so many frowns and sighs and I was getting antsy.

"So, what did he say? What's the sketch?"

Tim finally turned to me.

"He figured that we could probably approach the Tepui that we saw with about seven to ten days in the jungle beating trail. He would need two other guides to help him and would want to charge us something in the region of four hundred dollars to get us in."

Sick with gloom, Tim and I were shown to a place in the corner of one of this family's three open huts where we could set up our hammocks for the night. Christmas was only a few days away and I had already lost the will to continue struggling. We'd poured our hearts into this venture but had continued to get absolutely nowhere. Before bedding down for the night, we received a visit from our beaming host. He seemed to have taken a shine to Tim and offered to take him on a day hike into the adjacent rainforest for a little hunting and gathering. I planned to lie in my hammock all day and skulk hard. This I did, while fending off the inevitable hordes of voracious mosquitoes. When that following evening rolled around, my haul bag was already re-packed for the journey back to the village near the paved road. I intended to set off at first light on a mission to seek out some kind of Christmas spirit. Tim would follow at a more relaxed pace a little later.

My solo hike went well initially, with many landmarks along the way still fresh in my mind. When I reached the river crossing however, I set my camera's self-timer and plunged into the torrent for a manly portrait picture. Having accomplished this, I hoisted the heavy bag back onto my shoulders. The pig weighed in at well over a hundred pounds and was far from comfortable. Both waist and chest straps had lost their buckles, so I had knotted them together tightly before taking the plunge and proceeded with long, steady strides across the river to the other side.

The swirling water rose above my waist and then up to my chest. I was in midstream and struggling a little too hard, when suddenly and without warning, the river floor dropped away from beneath my feet, and I sank to the bottom. Huge bubbles of air escaped from the bag behind my head, quickly turning the huge bag into anchor-like, dead weight. Terrified beyond belief, I felt my feet and knees hit the bottom. Without a second thought, I gathered myself into a crab-like crouch, moved two paces, released and sprang for the surface. I felt both arms break free of the surface and search frantically for the bank, for anything at all. Once again, the monster pack was dragging me backwards and downwards towards the bottom. As I sank back beneath the water, my clawing fingers wrapped securely around the submerged roots at the river's edge, allowing my mouth to clear the water for one, endless gasp for air. Saved by a miracle. Soon I was fighting to gain purchase on the steep, crumbling bank above, fueled by an insatiable desire to live and tell. Up on the bank, the shock of what had just happened came quickly though, and as I lay panting in the long, tall grass, my upper body convulsed uncontrollably.

The near drowning had happened so fast that it took me a while to realize that the river had risen at least four feet unexpectedly. I had been so busy with my manly photo shoot that I had failed to notice this, a mistake that had very nearly cost me my life.

I began a long vigil for Tim's approach to warn him of the dangerous crossing.

A little later, we re-united with folks at the cheerful, roadside village and settled down to soak up a few cold and much needed beers. The campsite had filled up with tourists, almost overnight it seemed. Many of these families had journeyed all the way from Caracas to enjoy this unique area. We found an ample dosage of Christmas spirit while enjoying such great singing and hospitality as any place could afford.

In the aftermath of these festivities, we returned to Santa Elena, to once again mope around the bars and cafeterias like a lingering, alcoholic plague. In any event, word had spread of Tim's mugging epic. Many of the locals were sickened by the wrongdoing and felt obliged to offer their sympathy or somehow make amends for the injustice. We would always give our heartfelt thanks, but frustration and worse, indecision, would always resurface only to be subdued by jugs and jugs of cold beer. What would it take to change this run of really shitty misfortune?

The tides turned and things started to take a slight turn for the better when Tim broke down and called his father in Atlanta to request a five-hundred-dollar loan.

"Don't worry about a thing son; I'll have that money wired to you within the week."

Later that afternoon, we befriended an American gold smuggler living in exile. He seemed amicable enough and had many outlandish tales to share with us as he shepherded us across town to the one bar that we had not yet discovered, a large pool hall accessed by a long flight of stairs. Beyond the bustling pool tables, double doors led out to a narrow balcony overlooking the street. We grabbed our beers from the bar and sidled over to a table outside. After a while, I noticed a look of concern on Tim's face. He hadn't spoken a word since we had entered the place.

"Tim, what's wrong? You look like you've seen a ghost."

"That big guy over there by that table in the corner. I think he's one of the bastards who attacked me."

"Holy Christ. How can you be sure?"

Tim had remembered a cannabis leaf necklace that had been worn by one of his attackers. This guy was wearing the very same. He was also sporting a fresh dark bruise along the side of his right eye.

"That's him. I'm dead sure of it."

A few minutes of inner turmoil passed by before Tim rose silently from his seat and without a word, marched off in the direction of the La Guardia Nacional Headquarters.

Now it doesn't take a genius to figure out the follies of tangling with the Venezuelan National Guard. My fears were confirmed when, a little later, I peered down from the balcony to discover that everybody had fled the street and clumps of bystanders were now peering nervously from within crowded shop doorways. A brutish squad of machine-gun toting soldiers marched side by side down the center of the street towards us.

The ominous crash of heavy boots on the stairs caused everyone to freeze in time.

The door burst open and in they came. Guns were cocked and orders barked, with some fifty odd people jostled into a line up against the back wall. Believing myself to be somehow immune from all this excitement, I failed to comply in time, but the jab of a gun in my ribs and a rough shove sent me scurrying to join them. Tim was now ordered to identify the perpetrator. This he did. Without another word, the soldiers hauled him away, presumably to be interrogated, prior to being beaten into some kind of crimson mush.

That night, back at our guest house, Tim confided to me that he no longer felt safe in this town. "Strappo, something bad is going to happen to us. I can feel it. We need to get out of here, and soon!"

But our luck was about to turn full circle.

The next morning, as Tim and I snoozed away the last of our drink induced comas, there came a loud knock on our bunkhouse door. The knock jolted us awake like a cannon shot above the steady rumbling of monsoon rain upon the corrugated tin roof. Framed inside the doorway, the aviator spent a moment sizing us up before cracking the warmest of smiles.

"Buenos Dias. My name is Raphael. I will fly you both into La Gran Sabana for half price and you can pay me later. You like??"

And the man could drink too. Later that afternoon, he drove us across the Brazilian border to his favorite backstreet beer joint to douche our gullets.

No one could ever cross paths a more animated or passionate soul than this man.

Story had it that a year earlier, he had enthusiastically greeted his friend's pickup truck by swooping down low in his plane and slapping his wingtip on the cab roof, sending a chunk hurtling far across the landscape. Unperturbed, he landed on the rutted dirt road and tossed the wing piece into the cockpit before once again resuming his journey, leaving the occupants damp with fright.

By mid-afternoon, we were packed and ready once again. Once aboard, I also felt the dampness as Raphael's aerial hotrod meandered idly down to the starting grid.

And suddenly we were off. The plane hurtled down the runway, rocketed skywards and banked into a heart-pasting turn, with only cockpit glass between two bulging eyeballs and the jungle's outer walls far below.

We leveled out at cruising altitude and took stock of our surroundings. Beneath an azure sky, infinite carpets of untracked rainforest stretched out in all directions.

Distant highlands were crowned by vast big walls. Occasional plumes of drifting smoke signified the presence of Pemon settlements on the occasional patches of savannah grassland.

Soon, all eyes were fixed dead ahead at the vision that unfolded before us. From far away but closing fast, we cast our eyes on the unmistakable profile of Apauray Tepui. A perfectly symmetrical, coffin-shaped monolith, perhaps a mile in length.

Our tiny aircraft ran rings around the summit plateau as Tim and I scoped in vain for possible lines of weakness on the marble smooth and seemingly featureless walls. Thickening swirls of mist soon precluded safe viewing and so we bulleted down from the clouds and collided with the red dust airstrip in the village of Wonken, four miles beyond.

Once safely reunited with the earth, we bid Raphael a warm goodbye then bartered a ride in the village Land Cruiser over to the home of Ms. Gloria Pena. A giggling swarm of kids poured through open doorways and descended upon our morass of gear like land-borne Piranhas.

Each chunk of gear was whisked into the house and stashed away. Soon we were sitting with Gloria on the bench outside, chatting amicably as we warmed to each other's company. The number of adopted kids in her family was a fitting testimony to the greatness of this big-hearted lady.

Tim conveyed our intention to climb the neighboring rock. This concept was so alien to her indigenous mind that she visibly recoiled at the thought.

Not one to beat around the bush, Gloria launched into us.

"Why would you risk your lives in such a stupid way? Are you now telling me that you don't have rifles? What about Pumas? What about snakes? Do you really want to die?" By the look on her face, she obviously considered us to be naive and a little misguided, but her mind was already made up. Tomorrow would be New Year's Eve. Despite this, she would accompany us on our trail-breaking jungle approach up to a possible base camp beneath Apauray. Furthermore, a suitably armed guide would also be provided.

After dinner I retired early, slinging my hammock in a vacant corner of the room and settling in for the night. Since leaving Santa Elena, I had been keen to check a certain part of my anatomy. For some reason my toes had started throbbing quite painfully, but now was not the time, for tiredness quickly washed over me and I drifted away into another tired and dreamless sleep.

But that same vague worry resurfaced the following morning. Weird this, I pondered, as they wiggled back at me from the end of my hammock, barely visible in the grey prelight that crept quietly into our cold stone room.

A cockerel shrieked out his alarm call from far across the savannah and was soon joined in rhythmic chorus by many more. Sunrise was less than a block away.

Sticky with sleep, I rolled from my bed and hobbled across to the rickety old door, carefully weaving through a slew of hammocks amid the angelic snoring of sleeping kids. I emerged from the semi-darkness as a first thumbnail blaze of sunlight coated the mist-enshrouded grasslands with hints of gold.

I was spellbound, for out on the horizon; the squat profile of Apauray was also trapped in the blaze, a medieval castle towering above the vast moat of an inky jungle carpet.

In a few minutes the Land Cruiser would arrive to take us to visit the village elder. This was to be quite a momentous occasion, for we would need his permission before we could so much as approach the Tepui.

But first the toes.

I neglected to mention earlier that I had met a woman back in Santa Elena.

Maria was taking time away from her family and her devotion to marathon running. She was playing tour guide to a bunch of foreign tourists wishing to hike the arduous trade route up the largest of the Tepuis, Roraima.

We had met at a restaurant and drank, danced, and chatted until very late, then closed the evening with plans for a dawn jog out to the Brazilian border. This had been a stupid mistake on my part, because in my effort to impress Maria, I had forgotten that my choice of footwear lay with either rubber sailing boots or a pair of ten-dollar street shoes. This was exactly why my middle toe tips now looked like small black grapes.

Once settled on the bench outside the house, I absently peeled back the band aids that protected the battered toes from further wear and tear and examined two things. First, the nicely healing blisters, then some small, white lumps, each containing a tiny, pin-sized hole in the middle. I counted seven beneath my toenails, one in my chest and one in my hand. To my abject horror, I suddenly notice a wiggling maggot peeping at me from inside each hole. I want to be sick, but in view of the gathering crowd of enraptured onlookers, I opted instead for a prolonged wailing and gnashing of teeth as I tried in vain to eject the wriggling larvae from the many toe-holes. Beside me, a grown man turned away, but presumably not in disgust, for his quivering frame betrayed the fact that he was about to wet himself with laughter. How irritating! It would seem that the sight of a modern gringo whining about foot larvae will trigger just this type of reaction.

Unperturbed and with a dignified head held shoulder high, I ejected the maggot chunks from within the temple of my toenails.

I soon learned from Gloria that these horrific bugs are known as 'Níguas.' They were caused by biting sand fleas which are often found in the sandy areas close to rivers. I surmised that I had picked up these unwanted guests near the site of my near drowning episode. They become dangerous if left unattended, as they can enter the bloodstream and travel slowly and painfully towards the heart. Amputation of the affected limb can be the only lifesaving treatment at his point.

The truck arrived. With no time for any kind of breakfast, we threw on shoes and shirts, piled on the many packs of gear and clambered aboard.

Ten minutes later, we arrived at the home of the village elder. He was a wise and quite knowledgeable gentleman who quizzed us hard about our proposed plans. He demanded to know exactly what we intend to leave behind as anchors after reaching the summit.

We assured him that we would do our utmost to leave minimal evidence of our ascent. He consented, but only after much humming and haring, followed by a definitive handshake. Much relieved, we hopped back in the truck and beelined towards the jungle's perimeter.

Besides Tim and I, our team also included Gloria, a guide named Jorge and his shy, unassuming sister. Jorge wielded an ancient musket that appeared to have been borrowed from some museum somewhere. He seemed to be far too young to venture away from the relative safety of the savannah, but Gloria believed in him and so Tim and I maintained a diplomatic silence.

After a few parting photos, we hoisted our safari to our backs, hopped the gate and forged a trail through the undergrowth wall and into an altogether different kind of world.

With the fading of ambient light beneath a darkening canopy came the curtain call for a dramatic crescendo of bird and bug noises. Jorge headed the team, and I trailed along in mystical wonder a short way behind. As senses readjusted, out popped a little surface paranoia. My eyes cast furtive glances towards the trail behind me, seeking out the kind of imaginary cat that might stalk; the kind that might physically kill me and then drag me off and devour me in small, bite-sized chunks.

"Oh, yoo-hoo. Can I go in the middle" I quipped.

After a solid hour's hiking, the vague trail ended at an abandoned hut and we stopped for lunch, very glad of the rest and to take stock of our new surroundings. Somewhere, much higher up the hillside, Apauray loomed. The ground above was too steep to afford any kind of view. As Tim and I speculated upon possible lines of ascent, Jorge drew his machete and set off into the dense thicket, with only the rustling of foliage and an occasional 'zing' of the blade to alert us to his whereabouts. Tim and I followed meekly behind, tying ribbons of brightly colored surveyor's tape to select trees, in the vague hope of finding the trail again upon our return. During our many spells of inactivity, Gloria alerted us to a variety of dangerous-looking ants, stinging plants and some dazzlingly beautiful butterflies.

Soon we arrived at a fifty-foot band of mossy, slime-covered craprock. There was no choice now but to fix a guide rope up and over this obstacle. Poor Gloria: she was now in way over her head and so I belayed her safely back down and escorted her back to the deserted hut. Before we parted company, Gloria turned to face me and with a cunning variety of hand gestures, she described a blowout feast to honor our return to the village in a week's time.

Unburdened by the pack, I quickly rejoined the others. Gloved hands became the key elements of ascent as the ground steepened to a point where my plastic soled sailing boots became worthless on the slippery mud floor. Soon I was using knees and even the occasional elbow in a sweat-pouring, heart thumping jungle swim fest.

The angle finally eased, and we arrived abruptly at the edge of an abandoned clearing. It was getting late so Jorge and his sister departed, leaving us to gaze blankly out at a once significant world, now a long, long way below us.

The reality of our situation quickly became apparent when a torrential cloudburst hit the jungle, forcing us to slave like demons to set camp and stash away the gear.

Finally, we were able to crawl into luxurious sleeping bags and marvel at the thunderous rainfall and constant flashes of sheet lightning outside the tent. The rain eased to a steady drumming and lulled us towards a deep and premature sleep, and we failed to let in the New Year by four and a half hours.

January 1st.

"God, I need a vacation."

Outside, only the faintest of predawn bird and bug murmurings. Out in the forest they heralded the grey glimmerings of the New Year. It filtered through the tent walls and silhouetted an unsettling array of insect life milling about, eagerly searching for their newly arrived treats on feets.

Tim sat up with a low, nasal groan and began reinstalling his soggy, mud-caked clothes back over an equally stinking body. I lay back and stared at the blood in my eyelids.

"Me too. I'm totally knackered."

Suddenly a nearby sound pervaded upon sleep-dulled senses, like the steady comforting hum of worker bees snooping around a summer's rose garden.

With the noise came immediate rising panic, for the tent soon turned dark with bees and the noise outside resembled that of a small generator.

"Christ. What do killer bees look like?"

Don't know, but let's take a look anyway."

Tim slowly unzipped a portion of the tent door, allowing a few specimens to enter and be examined. They appeared to be relatively harmless sweat bees, but still we exited the tent with caution and backed slowly away.

In our rush to avoid the previous night's soaking storm, we had pitched the tent next to a tall, smooth-sided tree with a solitary knothole thirty feet up, that now billowed bees like a dense black smoke.

After a distracting breakfast comprising coffee, pancakes and bees, Tim and I readied ourselves for the unescorted trail-bash up to the base of the wall. This unpleasant but relatively short section would cost us two solid days of exhausting work.

During the fly-by inspection with Raphael, we had noticed that the jungle appeared to thin down to what seemed like a simple field of ferns on the final slope. Not so. As we left the forest, the joy of near success was tempered by the fact that these body length ferns were also festooned with a webbed tangle of dense, hardwood branches. Branches that a machete could barely even scratch. Three hundred yards of this took us eight grueling hours.

The heat thickened as we emerged from the jungle and into the glare of the mid-afternoon sun. Well blackened and bloodied, we marked time and began thirty-minute shifts of frenzied hacking as we inched our way up through the ferns to the base of the wall.

During one of Tim's stints, I maintained the necessary safe distance from an accidental swipe of the blade. While cowering in the shade, I gazed out across the ancient and primeval landscape, imagining a time long ago when huge, crane-necked dinosaurs and terrible winged carnivores ruled the earth. If ever there could be a place in our wildest dream to rekindle the essence of these long-forsaken creatures, it would be right here.

Far off in the distance, I spied other vast, monolithic plateaus, perhaps thirty miles away.

Each Tepui was resplendent with the silver eyelashes of freshly formed, overnight cataracts. I was awestruck by the realization that these waterfalls must be at least 2000' in height and having been fed only by localized storms, would probably disappear just as quickly.

Suddenly, a chilling scream sliced down through the slim corridor of the freshly cut trail.

"Tim?" Fearing snakebite, I bounded upwards and arrived to find him sitting in the ferns nodding to and fro and clutching his face. He informed me that the machete had connected with a rock, bounced back, and cut right across his face, possibly bisecting his right eyeball.

"Come on, let's have a look." The poor guy was badly shaken, feared complete blindness and was not at all cooperative.

I pried his hand away and examined the damage. Incredibly, the blade had been so dull that it had inflicted only a superficial lesion across part of the face and eyelid. Vision slowly returned to the swollen eye and despite renewed redness, it continued to maintain function.

We continued to thrash our way up the final fifty feet of dense brush and with huge whoops of delight, slapped our hands upon the prehistoric rock wall. Elated beyond measure, we spread-eagled our backs against the warm rock, allowing exhausted gazes to spiral skywards. Contented smiles were soon replaced by sullen scowls however, as we came to realize that the wall above was totally devoid of any cracks and not at all promising. Roaming the face with binoculars in both directions, we discovered nothing but smooth, featureless walls separating evil drainages choked with vegetation and poised rubble. Traversing along the base of the wall was soon deemed futile with the appearance of sudden, unexpected drop-offs lurking beneath the undergrowth at foot level. Our only hope now seemed to be to veer off from our existing trail lower down and hack our way over to a potential crack system around the corner. With this idea I mind we dumped our loads and headed back to camp.

It had seemed like a workable plan at the time, but the next day's foray was such a waste of time as to be laughable.

We followed our freshly cut trail up to the steepening below the ferns and then attempted to contour leftwards, but soon ran into completely impenetrable deadfall. We returned to camp somewhat defeated, knowing that our only chance of success lay in one of the vile corner systems up near the equipment that we had stashed beneath the wall.

In the days to come, we acclimated to the bees, the ants and the vague unease of jungle life while laying siege to a particularly nasty corner system rising into the ever-present monsoon mists.

The foul monsoon weather lingered on as we grappled with appalling conditions amid a continuous barrage of heavy rainstorms. Gloved hands became sponge white and painfully cracked as we peeled away grossly unpleasant carpets of waterlogged grass in an effort to slowly gain height.

Attempts to escape the clutches of the dank, seeping corner were futile. Solid cracks were non-existent in the sidewalls and most of the pins we did place held little more than mere bodyweight, tending to shift when weighted by the climber and causing many moments of near panic. Tim and I swapped leads four different times on this long aid pitch to allow frayed nerves some chance to rebirth.

On the third day, victory was suddenly ours as we finally broke free from the confines of the grotesque corners.

All the joys of our hard-won successes would soon be cut short by that unexpected meeting with our foul-tempered Vulture. Starvation became an exquisitely well-timed excuse and yes; we were more than ready to turn our backs on this adventure and get as far away as possible. We would try to forget about jungle wall-climbing, at least for a while.

Without more ado, we fixed our sixty-meter rope, rappelled back down into the jungle, and located our vague trail. It was getting late now, and we would have to move fast if we wanted to get clear of this forest before nightfall set in. We stashed harnesses and heaps of hardware back into the bags and headed down. Minutes later we were mudsliding down through the steaming foliage below. While roaming around the dark forest, we had always made it a practice to each carry a short branch and make enough noise to ward off any unwelcome critters. The clack of our warning sticks sounding against passing trees became muted and eerie in the forest's perpetual twilight. Eyesight was on full sensory alert for the usual nasties; the ants, the triple-edged razor vines and of course the snakes. Imagination was shameless and knew no bounds as I conjured up unsettling thoughts of warring tribesmen, a pouncing Jaguar or maybe a fat constricting snake, poised in mid-dangle and readying for the death strike. Tonight was different however as my focus was constantly drawn back to the Vulture and the fact that we'd been effectively barred from any further progress on the wall.

Lost in my thoughts I awoke as the trail landed us abruptly at the edge of the clearing. Tucked away in the back was our tiny lean-to composed of branches and banana leaves and next to that, our squalid little tent. Both shelters were covered in an array of stinking wet clothes. These in turn were alive with swarms of black sweat bees. The constant deafening drone would have been annoying at one time but life in the jungle had blessed us with a healthy indifference.

Wasted, we flopped down on a nearby log and ravenously devoured the very last remnants of our food supply.

"I may have to fly back to Santa Elena and borrow a pistol so I can waste that vicious prick, "I croaked, spluttering mouthfuls of Con Carne at Tim.

"Hey. Don't sweat the duck problem Strappo. It's my turn to lead and I'll punch it's lights out if it so much as winks at me."

I was a little doubtful. The encounter really troubled me, for I was beginning to realize that in the scheme of a typical rainforest we had clearly entered the realms of the expendable. Of course, all the clues were there to be missed, but it hadn't escaped my notice that any local villagers who ventured into the rainforest would always travel in groups and at least one would carry a rifle. Tim and I had just spent our first week alone and unarmed and the vague uneasiness of becoming a menu item for a higher order on the food chain once again prompted cravings for a much less dramatic world.

We quickly grabbed sleeping bags and a few personal items and resumed our journey. We still had a long slog ahead of us before we could exit the forest and cross the four miles of rolling savannah back to the village. We located our brightly colored marker ribbons and were soon slipping and sliding, ever spiraling downwards, until the track became ill-defined, causing us constantly back track to check our route. We stumbled onwards, boosted by ravenous appetites and a severe longing for friendly faces.

Later that evening we entered the village and as promised, Gloria and the kids pulled together an impressive dinner of chicken and rice in celebration of our unlikely survival. People flocked to the table as Tim recounted the epic tale of our bird encounter to an ever-changing sea of wide-eyed and attentive faces.

We spent a couple of soothing days loitering around the village. The locals sold us a little of what provisions they had, mainly small cans of tomato sauce and a little pasta.

Nourished and well rested, we returned to our jungle camp and resumed our assault the following morning.

Always a relief to rise above the forest, we re-ascended our fixed rope to arrive at the high point.

Tim selected his weapon, a lance-sized tree branch and then proceeded to hoist himself up on to my shoulders as I hung wincingly from the solitary bolt inside the chimney.

Deeply nervous, he sent the tip of his branch probing towards the deep horizontal cleft above, and elicited the same low, menacing growl that in deep vulture talk probably meant something like; "Bring it on motherfucker!" This caused a long enough pause in Tim for both of my arms to go completely numb. Tim growled back and while vigorously pounding his branch against the rock, started to swear in Spanish. From above, more growling, spitting, hissing, and wing beating from bilingual Big Bird was in turn greeted by more stick tapping and obscenities from below.

The standoff continued for twenty highly demented and nerve-wracking minutes. During this time, Tim stepped off my shoulders and onto my head, all the while bobbing and swiping with the branch. The beak arced down and swiped low, but somehow, amid all the yelling and thrashing, Tim stubbornly gained ground and sent one very irate Vulture scurrying deep inside the cleft.

Ecstatic, almost pant-wetting relief.

"You don't get that in the rock gym," came a faint chuckle, as he anchored himself into the cleft a good safe distance beyond the bird.

"O.K. You're on belay!"

Moments later I am tiptoeing past a ridiculously over-sized nest. I paused to gaze towards the source of renewed growling. Back in the dark, shadowy bowels of the cleft I caught sight of the one eye and my heart missed a beat. I literally sprinted over to Tim and arrived at the belay drained of anything remotely resembling courage.

We had now traversed sideways for at least half a rope length as we searched in vain for a weakness in the bristling overhangs above the break. Twice, I tried to strike some kind of pose on the wall above, but a lack of protectable cracks always had me scurrying back down to the safety of ledges in the cleft. We continued rightwards along the break for another hundred feet and Tim led a short difficult aid pitch over to the tip of a huge, vegetated pillar. The long horizontal cleft ended here, but fortunately so did the overhangs above us. It was decreed that our last stand would be performed right here. The rest of the day was spent feeding some initial placements into the unlikely-looking wall above. We cleaned off some ledge space on the pillar, fixed our rope back down to the ground and beat a new trail back along the base of the wall to our previous stash point.

Back in camp we re-examined our food situation and realized that starvation would again rear its ugly head in only two- or three more-days' time. We had a greater problem than food supply though, for the blank-looking wall above the pillar made a mockery of our efforts. Desperately thin nailing limited our next day's progress to a mere thirty pathetic feet.

We now had no choice but to travel light, sleep on the wall and at least try to finish the pitch. Foolishly, I opted to carry nothing warmer with me than a ratty foil space blanket and suffered the consequences.

We arrived at the tip of the pillar bright and early the following morning.

Once again, progress was mentally wearing and incredibly slow as the blank Pre-Cambrian sandstone extolled every known technique in our quest to gain height. Shallow indentations were scrupulously cleaned to allow for dicey cam or shallow pin placements. Hooks saved us many times over and limited the number of rivets drilled to just two. This was an ordeal in itself, as the compact rock dulled our drill bits, rendering them completely useless.

A crimson sun melted onto the distant horizon like spilt ice cream upon a hot, grey Sabana floor as we settled in for a cramped and uncomfortable night on the pillar. Later that night, a blinding storm moved in, and we thrilled to the joys of lavender sheet lightning, crashing thunder and torrential rain. A waterfall soon formed above me, and I wiled away the night with violent body shakes and uncontrollable shivering. By daybreak I was feeling the onset of mild hypothermia and fainted like a wuss upon standing up. An hour's basking in the fierce equatorial sunshine soon baked my innards to a point where I was good to go. I ascended to the high point and completely amazed myself by free climbing blindly out leftwards to top out at the next series of ledges on the wall. Tim cleaned the pitch and we both assembled at our new high point with some very mixed feelings.

Once again, our food had all gone. Drills were blunted and useless and so any future drilled anchors were out of the question. More importantly though, the much hoped for easing in angle and difficulty was a total mirage, for above us were naught but more impossible ceilings. A tuft of grass high up on the right skyline might be something to head for, certainly a long shot at best, but it may, just may, signify a real easing. Sadly, Tim informed me that he might never return to Venezuela, for he was soon to head back to his hometown of Atlanta to begin a doctorate.

I thought back upon all the hardships that we had just faced together in this new and often alien environment. At almost every moment there had been a struggle of some kind, be it heat, bugs, perpetual hunger, thirst or even the occasional stretch of hard, unprotected climbing. However, we had always managed to overcome those many hardships and keep forging ahead. That was, up until this now, for there was no doubt in our minds that we were now truly and soundly beaten.

During this prolonged moment of introspection, my mind cleared, and I suddenly understood what I must do. I made a solemn vow to myself. No matter what happened, I would return and finish what we had both started together and summit this Tepui.

We struck a deal. Tim would sell me his 8.5mm static rope which we'd anchor to our new high point and drape down the right side of the heavily vegetated pillar. It stopped short of the ground by about a hundred feet and so we tied a loop in the end and rappelled to the ground from here via our doubled lead rope. On the way down I paid careful attention to the grotesque chimney next to me, for I would need to climb back up and secure the end of the static line when I returned. In its current bone-dry state, it looked to be quite straightforward to me, but as with everything else around here; if it doesn't look too bad initially then watch out, for you're probably in for the fight of your life.

Caracas Airport.

With a violent, spirited handshake, Tim and I said our goodbyes and went our separate ways, never to see each other again. I was sad to see him go, for we had met as strangers and had bonded well. We had risked our lives together, reveling in more than our fair share of misery, but still we had rarely argued and now we parted as great friends. Still, it was time to move on.

Despite our failure, I arrived back in the States feeling mentally vibrant and sickeningly full of the joys of life.

Unfortunately, I was also homeless and on the flattest bones of my ass, having only $150 to my name and no means towards any ongoing travel back West.

Stranded at Miami airport, I foolishly attempted to hitch-hike back to Colorado.

Mr. Shifty pulled over and offered me a ride to the nearest beach. I declined his dubious offer. Having got nowhere with this scary tactic, I ended up crying out my woes to a big-hearted black lady at the Greyhound bus terminal desk and she dug around and came up with a hugely discounted bus ticket to Denver. Bless her. After buying some basic survival food my liquid assets were limited to a whopping six dollars; to be hoarded and later spent on cask conditioned ale, if and when, I did finally make it back to Boulder.

Three days later and stiff as a butcher's dog, I bade farewell to bus travel and swanned into the nearest brew pub for those well-earned pints.

Oblivious to the crowds of people swarming around my table, I mulled long and hard upon what might lie beyond the elusive tuft of grass and more importantly, how I might return to find out.

As I found a footing in my previous hum-drum existence, couch-surfing and abject poverty slowly gave way to some well-paid carpentry work and a temporary roof over my head.

When most needed, there could be nothing more satisfying than finding regular earnings, four familiar walls and a cozy bed to sleep in.

Within only a month however, I was solvent again and the vicarious thrills of a settled life were already beginning to wear off.

I began to look around for potential partners to accompany me back to Venezuela and

I preached to everyone within earshot about the magical wonders of La Gran Sabana; of a tantalizing tuft of grass high up on a mountain almost climbed.

Fortunately for this story, most of my friends drank.

In the same brewpub a few weeks later, my story sparked the interest of two of my 'alcoholically challenged' and therefore quite vulnerable friends.

Hector Padilla was my closest climber/carpenter/ boozer colleague. We had equivocal lifestyles, always finding ourselves in a similar array of travel misadventures. Venezuela would be just another part of the crazy lifestyle that we shared.

Hector had already lived in Northern Venezuela and was fluent in Spanish.

Yon Accio was the head bartender at the pub. He was completely untraveled, but was a fanatically dedicated climber, with an unquenchable; "Out of the way, I'll handle this!" attitude and youthful enthusiasm that usually won through.

So once again, frenzied preparations for a return trip got under way. Tickets to Caracas were purchased, but the untraveled Yon would have to follow us out a little later due to work commitments. It was decreed that Hector and I would await his presence in the central town of Cuidad Bolivar, a lively Orinoco River town and convenient halfway point in the twenty-one-hour bus ride from Caracas down to Santa Elena.

"Don't worry about a thing Yon, (titter), we'll leave you a note under a rock by the gate to the airstrip, telling you how to find us."

On my previous trip with Tim, just three months earlier, we had hopped off the bus in the dead of night and had then tried to sleep on the steps of this airfield. Deafening, discordant Christmas music had blared at us repeatedly from overhead speakers above the entrance, so we had sat on the steps and stared at every inch of that front gate until it opened at daybreak.

"We'll see you down there, y'ole git! Good luck and be safe."

Departure day arrived on a bright, snowy day in early April. Many vital, last-minute details were squared away.

Reeling with child-like enthusiasm, Hector and I boarded our first flight towards South America.

The journey kicked off with a minor but potentially disastrous drinking epic.

During the ensuing flights and our long layover in Houston Airport, Hector and I killed off sufficient brain cells to inflict massive retardation.

Exiting the plane like normal people wasn't even in the ballpark. We teetered unsteadily off the plane and into Caracas Airport with an overdramatic display of revolving kneecaps. Pretty soon I found myself spraying complete gibberish towards the bewildered customs and immigration officials with a hand placed over one eye to minimize double vision.

How the hell we made it into Venezuela defied all reason, but much later, with all gear bags intact and still in our possession, we stumbled off the bus in Cuidad Bolivar in a damp and dreary predawn, ashen faced and with all the plaintive vows of 'never again.'

Severe alcoholic poisoning only loosened its icy grip about the time that Yon found our note under the rock and tracked us down to the bustling Hotel Colonial two days later.

His only travel drama on the long solo journey had been having his passport stolen in Caracas and then bribing someone fifty bucks to get it back.

At any event, the witless quest towards the grass tuft continued with furious glee.

As we followed a familiar (to me) route southwards, I introduced and re-embraced many familiar faces along the way. With little time to catch our breath in Santa Elena, Raphael's busy flight schedule demanded that we fly into Wonken right away.

Gloria and the kids met us at the airstrip with huge smiles and directed us towards a newly constructed shelter composed of just four upright poles and a tin roof. It was situated on the outskirts of the village and afforded us a haunting view of the walls of Apauray Tepui.

The next day, all the thrills of mission involvement were tempered by towering backpacks and withering heat as we stumbled wincingly across rolling grasslands and into the enveloping jungle.

After a brief lesson on ant-life, we pressed onwards, eventually arriving at the much steeper trail leading to the old clearing that Tim and I had vacated, three months earlier.

Engrossed in this uphill trail bash, we paid little heed to the darkening patches of visible sky, until the sudden roar of a soaking squall drumming high in the canopy was followed by violent thunder boomers detonating right overhead. Lashing rain soon slowed upward progress to a crawl and forced us to jettison our heaviest loads, to be recovered later. Thus reprieved, we continued to a point where the slope eased. As we emerged into the clearing. blinking hard against the sudden light and pounding deluge, all eyes were cast skywards in the direction of the Tepui wall. Without warning, a loud crack exploded across the clearing and shook us to the core. A colossal tree, some hundred plus feet in height, crashed down and exploded right across our path, obscenely close to where my old campsite had been.

Fear ran rampant among us. I attempted to utter fake words of reassurance, but the utterance sounded weak and cloaked little of the unease I felt for the place, a kind of deep dread of yet one more unforeseen drama, the near fatal kind that is never seen or anticipated in time. All we can do is learn and adapt.

The rain passed and a measure of calm returned as we hacked out some extra flat space by the old site. We erected our township and bedded in for the night.

During a fitful sleep, I wrestled with unpleasant dreams and images of a frayed and bleached rope hanging next to a seeping, glistening chimney. Upon waking up, I had the strangest feeling that the epic had already been played out on Apauray, and that our future attempt was just some kind of movie rerun, with the outcome already set in stone.

We lounged around camp and ate a leisurely breakfast, while allowing our water-logged clothes to dry in the baking sun. Yon, however, brought to our attention his apparent aversion to bees by whirling dervish-like around camp and thrashing himself, and the occasional buzzing bee, with a branch.

Just a passing phase, we hope.

Unable to contain our curiosity any longer, we ascended to the wall with bated breath. Plant life on the trail had almost fully regrown in my absence, but the dense ferns were easily toppled, and our old path re-established. Yon beat us to it and eagerly scanned visible areas of rock amid curling wisps of mist above.

"Hey, I can see the rope. I see it!

A huge relief. Sure enough, still draped down the clean, sweeping wall just to the right of the pillar, a short, knotted loop beckoned at the end of my abandoned fixed line, stopping one hundred feet shy of the ground. Rounding the final corner though, I was appalled to discover that the once climbable chimney that would allow us to access the rope had been transformed by recent rains into the vilest drainage of them all. Oil dark walls and copious vegetation quietly trickling with water.

With feet skating wildly, I managed to clean out rubble and moss as per the norm. After struggling up to a tiny foot ledge, eighty feet up, I discovered that all further progress was barred by a horrific, hour-glass constriction composed of unattached, fridge-sized boulders.

"This is total death! There is no going around this! We may have to fail! I'm coming down."

We returned the next day, and I shimmied up to my high point once again, only to cower and quake beneath the same set of boulders. I let more time drift aimlessly by as I stared vacantly at the looped end of the fixed line, still twenty feet higher up. Plenty of time to sit and contemplate the shame of explaining this fiasco to all my friends back home.

Then, out of pure desperation, I hauled up a long, thin lodge pole tree trunk from the jungle floor and draped the tip with a selection of slings. The branch was heavy and required a big effort to raise it up. I was relatively secure though, with both feet planted firmly on a phonebook sized ledge and my lower back wedged against the chimney wall. After waiting for the return of blood to my forearms, I launched the tree vertically and with every quivering ounce of strength, began to hoist the tip skywards in the direction of the loop. Then, on the third tendon-shredding sweep, the open carabiner caught, and the loop was finally clipped.

The crags resounded with loud cheers and yells of delight; mostly mine.

By lunchtime, we were scarfing down energy bars at my previous high point, an exposed eyrie perched safely above and beyond the evil drainages, the bad-tempered bird, the unbreachable ceilings and of course the blank, desperate wall beneath us.

"Pretty impressive huh? That last ninety-foot pitch took us two and a half days to complete." I boasted, hoping for a little sympathy.

"You Nancy Boy. You'd better go quicker than that on the next pitch or we'll have you euthanized!"

Yon and Hector unraveled a double portaledge and reclined in perfect belaying comfort as I readied for the next pitch into uncharted lands.

Soon, I was engrossed in the subtle nuances of the virgin wall above, cleaning out soil and veggies from shallow, unappealing fracture lines before pounding in blade pins or birdbeaks. Every piece I placed quickly bottomed out and recoiled with a dull thud.

Bounce testing, the scary bit, would come next.

This technique is performed by setting a foot in the lowest stirrup that hangs from the newly placed piece. More and more body weight is transferred to the stirrup and if the piece still continues to hold, then a full-weight, white-knuckle launch is made to clip in, hang and breathe a prayer.

Rising slowly in this manner towards the tantalizing tuft, I skirted beneath the ceilings and traversed blindly around the skyline's edge to a point where I could, once and for all, caress its long fronds at the very limit of my reach.

Above, I could see absolutely nothing to ever commend my being back here. Of course, I should have known better than this, and like Tim, could have chosen to turn my back on this project months ago when I had the chance. Now I would have to keep shaming myself into pushing a bad position, rather than accept a defeat; after investing all this time, work, money, and fear.

Beyond the tuft, I could see nothing but continuously steep rock leading up to another blocky roof. This one was large enough to prevent any kind of scrutiny of the upper face, but did at least possess a deep, vertical crack splitting the rock into two sections. Lured by the promise of placing solid gear in the crack, I moved gingerly up to beneath the roof. To my dismay, I discovered that both sides of the crack resonated with a deep, bass drum boom when thumped, signifying the potential for dislodgment, and a cheese grating transformation of my body parts into a long red skid mark back down the face.

In the throes of blind fear, I started talking to myself. At length, we both agreed not to surrender, so I feigned lightness and gently hoisted myself over the roof crack while humming mindless tunes to myself and focusing solely on happy thoughts.

Once safely above the roof, my attempts at placing a solid anchor fell short when one of the two ¼" bolts buckled. Still muttering to myself, I threw in a couple of stout wires before bringing up Hector and Yon.

Now the wall dropped back to less than vertical but seemed to be composed of nothing but pure grass, the odd tree and almost no visible rock.

I just don't believe this, I sighed, saddened by the lack of any easing in difficulty.

After throwing on a pair of leather gardening gloves, I progressed up the appallingly exposed slope by grappling with armfuls of grass and chopping out the occasional secure foothold with the pick of my hammer. Quite soon, I was seventy feet above Hector and Yon with zero protection between us.

I recoiled from a much larger clump directly above my head and began to tremble quietly. The terrain below was too steep and crumbly to reverse, so I chose instead to bury my face and arms in the long grass above, very glad to tune out the oppressive, clinging void beneath my feet.

My hands inadvertently knocked over a dead, paper dry tree stump and suddenly, out poured an army of black, gel cap-sized ants. These aggressive bastards sported bright, scarlet underbellies and moved with great speed, sprinting along the taller leaves, and dropping onto my long sleeves and gloved hands. They doubled over in unison and upon raising their hind legs, commenced biting.

Terrified, I brushed them off and slithered a short way back down the grass wall with the angry, displaced ant pack in hot pursuit. The chase ended ten feet below when quite miraculously, they fanned out and took up positions on the tips of the long grass and began to quiver their long feelers in an agitated and quite alarming manner.

For forty-five calf cramping minutes, I stood dead still, clutching at the grass wall while keeping a watchful eye on these hostile, menacing ants while having no clue what to do next.

Finally, in a state of utter dread, I broke cover and in a high-speed flurry of thrashing arms and elbows, blundered past the nest and paddled my way up the final sixty feet of undergrowth. The grass became longer, suggesting a ledge and as I parted the fronds, I suddenly burst through onto a narrow oasis of flat ground. I parked myself next to a cool, refreshing cascade tucked away in the back.

Thoroughly spent, I flopped down and gazed uneasily at the dome-like summit rim high above. Before long, Hector and Yon arrived and offered plenty of much needed enthusiasm, but my spirit was fully jaded, clouded by all too vivid images of recent near disasters.

Far above, I could see nothing but bald, crackless rock amid the blinding glare of sun reflecting from streams of water trickling down from the summit plateau.

Initially, things start out nicely. I racked huge and grappled with cool, shaded corners rising from the oasis. But one hundred and twenty feet later, the corners vanished into blanker rock that reared up for one last steepening. I placed my last solid piece of protection deep inside a pocket and sauntered out rightwards across the seeping slabs, taking extreme care not to disturb the many detached islands of heavy, waterlogged grass. Once safely beyond, I unearthed a small, matchbook sized slot and inserted a mediocre camming piece before attempting to step up. No go. The slab above was veneered with a thin film of grease.

With the summit only a bus length away, blind frustration took over and in a ridiculous, last-ditch attempt, I sculpted my own personal foot ledge by installing a clod of wet grass at chest height and tamping it down into something vaguely flat.

It almost worked too.

As I slowly straightened up, eager to grasp beyond my range, the mudhold peeled away and I fell; braced for a sudden, ugly swing into the void, but only to be jerked to an abrupt halt by the nearby cam.

Badly shaken, I shuffled rightwards across the steep, unprotected slabs for another sixty nerve-wracking feet, desperately seeking a line to the summit, but finding none. Holding down the rising panic, I lurched to a higher line of holds, latched on, and then hauled my trembling body into a precarious standing position.

Not too bright that, for now there was no getting back down.

Suddenly, the rope tugged hard at my waist, almost dragging me backwards.

Fully crazed, I strained to resist, but then paused, for at the very limit of earshot, caught the faintest dual screams from far below.

"NO MORE ROPE!"

Mortified, I turned around and surveyed the irreversible rock surface sweeping away into a horrific unseen, convex void below. Now I had to face the prospect of a two hundred foot, arching death fall as I tried and failed to get back down.

But there was another way. Just one slim chance.

Six feet below and a body length away was a small ledge, about the size of a large cereal box. The rope was tight to my waist right now and ran horizontally back to my last placement, eighty feet away.

Got to do it.

In the last dying throes of despair, I grabbed the rope at arm's length like a vine in a Tarzan movie, but with only one scene and only one take.

Readying for the leap, knowing that if I overshot...

Bang! I swung across and both feet slammed squarely into the ledge, but the rope was now slack in my hands and I started to topple off backwards. Choked with terror, blind reflexes sent fingers lashing out in a flurry of movement; frantically clawing at the rock and then suddenly catching on something. No idea what, but now I had regained my balance. I failed to notice the plaintive, whimpering sobs escaping from my throat. Not until the heaving subsided and breathing returned to normal again.

Much later that evening, back in camp, I delicately broached on the subject of failure and escaping for good.

"As long as I live and breathe, I will never go near those slabs again. I very nearly died up there."

"Well? What goes on above those oasis corners? Surely a long, direct line to the top would be the way to go."

"Yeah. That might be our last remaining hope. There can be no other way."

Hector and Yon were probably right. The more I thought about it, the more I convinced myself that I should force that direct line to the top, despite my having vetoed the plan earlier in the day.

And so, at length, we make a pact; to return and attempt just one more shot at that direct route up to the summit.

The trauma of the near fatal accident persisted however, for when the next morning rolled around, I cowered in the face of unshakeable dread, keeping my tent door firmly closed.

"Piss off. Go away. I'm not coming out."

So instead, a calmer, more restful day was spent lounging around an oppressively hot jungle camp, swatting bees and trying to figure out what to do next. With a pressing need for some renewed resolve, we discussed and gradually diminished the many potential setbacks in our strategy. As nighttime rolled in, I adjourned to bed, readying myself for some serious conquering in the morning.

Our journey back up the fixed ropes the following morning was nerve-wracking and anything but straightforward. While passing across the detached roofs below the wall of grass, Yon discovered a serious fray in the rope's sheath and had to creep gingerly past, before making the passage safe for the rest of us.

We arrived at the oasis, and I ascended to the deep pocket high up beneath the final steepening. This time I was sporting a full-blown hula skirt, comprising every scrap of our climbing gear. Thus armed, I set off one more time into uncharted lands, bounce testing on absurdly shallow pin placements and focusing solely upon difficulties at face level.

Before long, I arrived at another deep pocket and finally had a chance to place some real protection. As I started scraping out dried soil prior to placing a secure camming device, a teeming horde of smaller, dark brown ants emerged, a species would come to be known to us as; 'The Slow Biters.'

As this latest standoff continued, I realized that sooner or later, I would have to make full use of the pocket, so as to free climb above and out of reach of the glistening swarm. Furthermore, I seemed to be catching grief from two happily bored and inactive hecklers from way down in the stalls.

"Oh. Please DOO-OO- hurry up, Wussy."

"Come on Shirley. They won't hurt you."

Chicken! Cluck, cluck."

For once though, I had solid protection right in front of me and any fall I took would be relatively safe. With this idea in mind, I threw a foot high up into the ant nest and lurched upwards, reaching and reaching… all the way to…Nothing.

As they came swarming up my legs and down my sleeves, the manic tickling of thousands of tiny ant feet began in earnest.

Helpless and completely spread-eagled on the rock and unable to take a hand off, the tickling suddenly stopped as the ants switched into slow, methodical biting mode.

Two choices. With only seconds to go before blood was drawn, I could either jump into the void or make one more harrowing step up.

The step worked and I fired in the first pin grabbed from my rack, clipped into it and began swatting furiously.

The summit was right overhead now as I continued to make headway for another twenty intricate feet. Below me, a string of bodyweight pieces, just aching to be unzipped if I fell.

Soon I was hanging from three different pins, with my weight carefully equalized to each one.

I barely dare to breathe.

More blankness above. A rivet would need to be drilled to make any further progress. I began to pound and twist the drill, until a tiny ¼" hole started to form. The rock was even harder up here and very quickly dulled, then flattened the tip, causing the drill bit to bounce back out. I pounded my rivet into a hole that was less than ¾" deep, then looped a wire over the head and stepped gingerly up into my stirrup. Now I had a clear, uninterrupted view of the very last sweep of rock leading right to the summit.

And this was precisely where I had to fail for the second time.

I still had sixty more feet of odious, black sandstone to surmount, but with rock that was much too slippery to free climb on, no visible cracks in sight and now not a hope in hell of placing even one more rivet.

A time to let all my frustrations come pouring out.

A time to weep quietly and inwardly.

This I did, while fixing ropes yet again, as I prepared to retreat back to North America for the second time.

Back down at the oasis, the shame of my defeat sank painfully in, with the unshakable feeling that I had just let the whole side down.

It gnawed at my belly like poison and sickened me to the core. Oblivious to Hector and Yon's attempted words of commiseration, I sat and moped dejectedly, while re-enacting the day's events over and over inside my head.

I concluded that this last part of the wall might never be climbed, at least not in its current, soaking wet condition.

Almost a whole year drifted by before we returned to Apauray Tepui and laid siege to that nightmarish sixty feet of rock. Hector and Yon were still keen to see this thing through, but this time we also managed to coerce and enslave a fourth player, Chad Goodchild.

Not surprisingly, the long trek back to Southern Venezuela seemed like such a lot of work. All that way, just to attend to one piddling chunk of cap rock.

At the last minute, we decided to alter our plans and instead, fly deeper into La Gran Sabana and reconnoiter another Tepui wall.

The Acopan plateau was a vast, largely unexplored region and typified the 'Lost World' that Sir Arthur Conan Doyle had so well portrayed in his book of the same name.

I had gazed at these distant walls; resplendent with their overnight cataracts while beating trail with Tim, during our first attempt on Apauray. Our curiosity was all consuming and the severe longing to merely stand beneath these remote cliffs was welcomed as an almost vital diversion. Anything to avoid that all too familiar slog back up endless fixed ropes, just to confront that black, summit wall of Apauray.

Acopan had been the scene of a serious climbing accident, some years earlier. A climber had slipped and fallen seventy feet, landing in the remote jungle with a badly broken leg. Being so far from any kind of help, his partner had undertaken a very daring rescue; trekking alone through the dense jungle at night and carrying his friend back out to await a plane ride out. In doing so, he had not only saved the victim's life, but also his badly infected leg from almost certain amputation. A small patch of flat ground had been cleared of rocks, to act as a makeshift airstrip. It remained as a grim reminder of this incredibly close call.

Raphael agreed to fly us into that same diminutive patch of grass but would be unable to take off with so much weight in his plane, due to the shortness of the runway. It was basically a one-way trip for us. This minor glitch seemed highly irrelevant though. Thanks to this unexpected twist in our adventure; our wimpish apathy had turned to a sudden and unshakable resolve.

All talk ceased as widening eyes fixated upon the tiny patch of unbroken grass below. We banked sharply into the final turn and landed with a heart stopping bounce as Raphael slammed on the brakes, bringing the plane to a shuddering halt, amid an impressive cloud of dust.

After unloading the gear and saying our now familiar farewells, the engine screamed at full throttle once again. He sent the plane rocketing skywards to slowly disappear into the horizon. Soon, the intrusive sound faded out, to be replaced by an absolute and disquieting stillness.

We were greeted by one of the locals and offered the use of a nearby hut as a staging ground for our operations.

His name was Leonardo, and we were surprised to note that he was decked out in climbing attire. We came to realize that he must have helped beat trail for the previous, ill-fated expedition. Senor Leonardo agreed to help shepherd us to the base of our chosen route.

This was truly incredible country. An austere wall of gold, some two thousand feet high, rose out from the steeply inclined jungle. Off to the side of the main wall, an area of bare grassland rose up to meet the cliffs. Swayed by the easy nature of this approach, we arrived at the base of Acopan's heavily vegetated wall two days later. We cast our gaze upon a familiar, uncompromising terrain and quickly realized that there could never be any 'quickie' climbing projects in La Gran Sabana. Furthermore, the steep open ground at the base was furrowed by a series of enormous J-shaped gouges, like giant, vertical skateboard ramps. It suddenly dawned on us that these furrows must have been created by run-off from the plateau high above. These would be the landing sites for those giant overnight waterfalls that we had seen from so far away. To commit to climbing the wall and then become vulnerable to such unbridled power and danger, suddenly gave us some real pause for thought.

After much deliberation, it was the fear of a sudden drowning death that swayed our decision to abandon our bold plan for a rapid ascent of Acopan.

We turned tail and marched our heavy loads all the way back through the open wilderness towards Gloria's village. These were brutally tiring days, for it had not rained in a long time and the ground was parched and dry, adding venom to an already searing, equatorial heat.

We arrived in the afternoon of the third day, only to be informed that a team of Venezuelan climbers had just flown into the village and had quickly marched up to the base of our route on Apauray Tepui.

In our exhausted state, we had hoped to recoup some nourishment and strength in the village. The long hike in appalling daytime temperatures was compounded with thoughts only of conserving our precious food supply. With little appetite anyway, the daily ration consisted merely of a mouthful of corned beef and a few boiled candies. We had been reduced to subsisting on whatever fat stores remained on our emaciated, withered frames.

But no rest for the wicked because this new revelation would have to change everything.

This was indeed strange news. We had met these climbers back in Santa Elena and they seemed like real decent guys. As far as I could recall, they had been involved in climbing on the walls of the giant Roraima Tepui. Unfortunately, their proposed route overlooked the main hiking trail and was highly visible to tourists and other passersby on the trail up to the summit.

I suspected that they must have attracted some undesirable attention from the National Guard and had been shut down. I couldn't help but feel a little uneasy though, for in such a vast wilderness as La Gran Sabana, why had they chosen to visit this particular wall? One with a line of fixed ropes leading almost to within spitting distance of the summit? My urgency to solve this mystery prompted a huge surge of frantic impatience bordering on near hysteria.

Early the following morning, my beleaguered colleagues were frog-marched across the savannah and ushered into the all too familiar jungle. Thanks to my impatience however, we lost the trail and wandered blindly into an area of dense, impassable ravines. It was only after back-tracking carefully away from these, that we accidentally stumbled into one of the Venezuelan climbers.

He informed us that; just as we had imagined, they had been ordered to cease operations on Roraima. His team was now living in a cave up near our fixed lines and would attempt to climb this Tepui.

With feigned enthusiasm, we arranged to meet with him the next day and departed this uncannily strange meeting for our old campsite in the clearing.

We arrived a little later, to discover that in our absence of eleven months, the tent-sites had re-grown, with thin-branched trees and bushes towering an amazing fifteen feet above us. Hours passed before we completed the camp restoration and retired for the night.

As we broke free of the forest and entered the ferns the next morning, our loud yodels were returned by the party below the wall. What we ran into as we followed the fresh trail beneath the cliffs stunned us beyond our wildest imaginations.

Had we cleared just fifty more yards of trail along the base, we too might have discovered the low roofed cave that now housed four grinning and contented Venezuelans. A droolworthy aroma of crepes and fresh brewed coffee greeted us as we turned the final corner and stumbled upon an immaculately groomed cook, replete with tall white hat and dressed in the crisply starched uniform of a cordon bleu chef. Having eaten just one real meal in the entire preceding week, the offer of crepes in syrup and sips of coffee not only almost triggered a near riot among us but cemented a solid bond of friendship between our two teams.

With Hector acting as interpreter, the lead climber, Sebastian, informed us that they had just attempted the same evil drainage that Tim and I had first cleaned and climbed a year ago.

"Had they run into an enormous, angry bird?" we enquired. Apparently not, but they had taken one look at the ceilings above and beat a hasty retreat.

With nothing better to do, they had taken a run up our ropes, discovering another serious fray in one area. After making it to the oasis and finding no line of ropes leading to the summit, they had returned to the base and were now involved in trying to figure out what to do next with their lives.

I already had the answer.

The gift of pancakes had to be returned, and without the slightest hesitation, I invited them to join us on our final bid for the summit. The offer was greeted at first with surprise, followed by warm, appreciative smiles. Without any further discussion, we distributed the racks of heavy gear and made tracks back up the ropes towards the oasis, and all that lay beyond.

This time, a little fortune smiled down upon our visit. I gazed skywards, suppressing the nagging dread of revisiting the same stretch of rock that had twice defeated me. It was not a mirage though. The entire wall was bone dry, and I could now free climb up towards my previous high point with relative ease.

Fifty feet up and I paused to focus on some sudden commotion back on the ledge below.

Chad was busy reliving one of those unforeseen dramas; the kind we all loathed and dreaded.

While engrossed in ascending one of the fixed ropes lower down; he had heard the unmistakable and terrifying sound of an approaching swarm of bees coming his way.

He swiveled around in time to watch a thick black cloud go rushing by him.

"For just one short moment, the sound was deafening. I was completely terrified," recalled Chad. Those on the oasis ledge had heard it too. Even from so far away, the unearthly buzzing had frozen everyone in their tracks, as the disquieting sound passed by and receded into the distance.

I approached my old high point and regained the shallow rivet, but only by reverting to the same methodical aid climbing. Between me and the overhanging cornice of thick, summit grass lay that final sweep of foreboding, dark sandstone. Renewed hope surfaced however, when I realized that the rock was still bone dry, even up here. There also appeared to be a vague sloping ledge, thirty feet higher up; something I hadn't even noticed on my previous ill-fated attempt. Blessed with this one hope, I launched blindly up on reasonable friction holds and arrived below the ledge with the familiar dread of another devastating fall, should I blow it. Fully committed, I now threw a foot high up and onto the sloper, then attempted to rock my weight over. There was nothing but a choked up crack off to one side. In a lightening reflex action, I thrust my whole arm into the crack and carefully stood straight up. Upon withdrawing my bare forearm from the crack, I almost cut loose with a barely stifled scream, and almost threw myself off the wall in blind panic, for my arm was now covered with the same oversized, scarlet-colored ants that I had run into down on the grass wall. These little bastards had their hind legs raised and were trying to dig through my skin. Miraculously, their size and bright color were only for show, and they appeared to be completely harmless. I felt very blessed, for I could never have maintained my precarious stance on the rock had they been otherwise.

With pure loathing, I brushed them off and continued to creep carefully upwards. Soon I was swimming through the final overhang of lush jungle, and then in one last, grass-grasping heave, stepped up and planted both feet firmly upon the level ground of the summit.

Overjoyed and relieved beyond any measure, I gazed at the verdant plateau of unseen and unrecorded plant life that opened out in front of me. As I moved to step forward, the rope held me back like a dog leash. Loud, urgent yelling from down on the oasis informed me that I was once again, completely out of rope. This presented another unwelcome dilemma, for now I was teetering at the brink of the Tepui wall, with the nearest tree to anchor to still fifteen more feet beyond my reach. After much pause for thought, I solved the problem by untying and fixing the rope to a medium-sized chunk of mushy, decomposed rock down by my feet. Any tug from below and the rope would have disappeared back over the edge. With an unspoken prayer to not let this happen, I joined every last scrap of climbing gear together to form a long chain and made it over to the tree with absolutely nothing left to spare.

"I'm safe! Jumar when ready!" Safe to breathe at last. I stepped back from the tree and savored my new environment while awaiting the arrival of the team.

Suddenly and without any warning, the dreaded sound of the bee swarm filled the air. Out of the corner of one eye, I saw them rising to the plateau, like a shroud from the depths.

With only seconds to act, I dropped down onto my knees, opened my arms and closed both eyes to a squint before being completely engulfed in the frenetic, rushing cloud of bees. In some instinctively cold and calculating way, I managed to remain calm; solid in the belief that unless forced against you, a bee will never sting you if you keep perfectly still. Whatever documentary I had watched may have just saved my life, for these large insects moved around my head with the arrow-like speed of tracer bullets.

A terrible time to test theories though, as I felt the urgent wing beats crawling all over my exposed flesh as I craned my neck ever so slowly, back towards the tree. The branches were now so thick with bees that the tree appeared to sway, as if blown by some imaginary wind. Self-control soon began to crumble away, as pure horror broke through my paralysis and instilled an overwhelming urge to bolt, to go crashing through the undergrowth in a last-ditch flight for life.

Just as this suicidal impulse churned into life, the deafening roar of the swarm magically rose up from the around me and faded into the distance. I tried to stand up, but my legs failed me, and I sank back to the floor.

And there I stayed, quietly shaking, as the first of the oasis crew arrived to dissolve my nightmare with laughter and whoops of blissful, triumphant joy.

In all, seven climbers summited the virgin plateau of Apauray Tepui. A multinational ascent to the end, comprising; a Brit, one Mexican/American, two Americans, two Venezuelans and a French/Venezuelan.

I couldn't help but wonder what might have happened if Yon had summited instead of me. Indeed, I had offered him the lead at one point, but he had declined. Yon was always prone to swatting bees whenever he got the chance. As I pointed out, these were not the harmless sweat bees that tormented us back in camp. They were over twice the size and seemed to be a lot more aggressive. What might have happened had I tried to outrun the swarm?

There are too many unanswerable questions. I'd just have to let it go.

It was easy to believe that some kind of mystical forces were at work, high up in these sacred places. Oddly enough, it had not rained a single drop during our entire stay in Venezuela. It was only this extreme dry spell that had made it possible for us to succeed on this last summit attempt.

After a prolonged lounging session on the plateau, we began the arduous roped descent back down the intricate wall. The unease of a jammed rope or occasional rockfall danger dissipated as the whole team dropped safely down the final rappel to the jungle floor. At the exact second that the last man touched down to the ground, the heavens open and a deluge of driving rain continued to pound us without end.

The discovery of a secret stash of beer in the village the following day gave rise to prolonged and boozy celebrations. The locals also provided us with horses, mostly for their own personal amusement, as these plucky little beasts sensed our ineptitude and made concerted efforts to catapult us back onto the ground.

Soon however, it was time to hug everyone goodbye and board Raphael's bullet plane back to Santa Elena; the first step in our long journey home. Much later that evening, the townspeople, both young and old, joined us for a night of raucous dancing, interspersed with whiskey shots and round upon round of beers.

I awoke on the bustling Saturday morning sidewalk at around 10am with my body and brain racked with pain. Worried that we might miss our assigned seating on the bus heading north, we had dumped our mountain of climbing gear next to the bus stop and I was duly elected to sleep right on top of the pile; a very uncomfortable and highly public place to reside, whilst making a complete spectacle of myself in full view of the entire town. The gang arrived and we boarded the streamlined, air-conditioned coach, bound for the north coast of Venezuela.

I disgraced myself again some hours later.

With curtains drawn to improve the A/C and no outside view, coupled with the ocean-like, rolling motion of the bus, extreme queasiness soon had me racing for the cramped bathroom cubicle at the rear of the bus. I failed to hit the toilet seat target by a mile, causing everyone to vacate the bus and await a replacement in the sweltering heat. By this time many of the passengers were just aching to shoot me in the head.

That near death experience awaited me in a dark alley about a week later.

We made it back to Caracas with only one more 'stomach' stop, this time on the grass verge outside of the bus. Next, we journeyed westwards along the rolling and windy Caribbean coastal road, to eventually track down and then stay with Hector's good friend, Emilio Sanchez. Emilio was the mayor of the town of Tucacas and showed us some cutting-edge hospitality, even assigning us a young 'security guard' known as 'The Vulture.' Two more friends flew in to 'assist' us with our celebrations, Mickey Trotter from London, and Cloy Coats from California.

One afternoon, after a substantial swilling session in Vulture's favorite dive bar, there came about a vague awareness that darkness had arrived outside, causing us to scurry with some urgency through the Barrio's dark alleys back to the safety of the busy, illuminated streets 300 yards away. Vulture suddenly decided to run back to his house to grab his cellphone. And then it happened. My would-be killer emerged from the shadows, pulled the slide back on his 9mm pistol and shoved it right up against my forehead, while yelling for my money. In a flash, Hector wheeled around on him and knocked the gun away from my head while screaming even louder obscenities. My assailant backed down and fled, just as the Vulture returned after hearing all the commotion. It was yet another incredibly close call that had come and gone in just a few nightmarish seconds. Hector later went on to inform me that while living in New York City, seven different scumbags had tried to mug him. He told me that he had always gone on the offensive when being attacked and had never been successfully robbed, (or shot), even to this day.

Hector's tactic may have well prevented some serious bloodshed and even a potential homicide.

The PTSD that followed did not in any way conform to it's original definition. Post Tepui Severe Drunkenness had become the norm, for Emilio had given us the keys to a palatial million-dollar mansion, allowing us to wile away the days, sipping cocktails by the pool and speculating on what to have for dinner.

Epilogue

One morning, Emilio asked us if we might help him deliver Red Cross food boxes to some of the more remote villages and towns inland. Apparently, there had been a disastrous spell of torrential rain and mudslides prior to our arrival and so we helped load up the battered old canvas covered lorry and then delivered said Cruz Roja boxes to off the beaten track towns until late into the night; to many families in dire need; in places that had rarely, if ever, seen a tourist.

The following morning, after our heart pumping sweat fest, it was time for us to raise an early morning glass of ice-cold beer to the Coffin shaped tepui just one more time. Out blurted the stoic, heartfelt farewells, before beginning our own separate journeys back to our respective lives of normalcy and everyday routine.

Without realizing it at the time, my life as a big wall expedition climber had finally drawn to a close.

Safely ensconced back in my everyday work life in Boulder many weeks later, lament and regret began to seep through the cracks.

I couldn't help but hark back to my most recent climbing excursion with darkness and suspicion.

What had I really achieved and at what cost?

After three grueling expeditions to Venezuela, all within the space of just eleven months, I'd actually scored some kind of mountaineering success: albeit just a mere jungly one.

But at what kind of price?

Just prior to my most recent trip I had also started to develop strong feelings for a wildly attractive, raven haired, witchy woman.

Julie and I had recently enjoyed a romantic first date in Sayulita, Mexico; along with her two daughters; nine-year-old Kashmir and thirteen-year-old Summer.

I'm not sure exactly why, but I had always been reserved and a little shy around children. In all my years, I had never really been around kids. I'd rarely, if ever, spoken to them. Nor had I ever held a baby in my arms. So, when we rolled through the door at Julie's mountain home near Nederland, Colorado after a long flight home, Kashmir, who'd had very little interaction with men in her life thus far, looked up at her mum and asked.

"Mom. We really like him. Can we keep him?"

Julie and I seemed to be made for each other and became inseparable, and so I happily morphed into the role of seriously devoted stepdad, almost overnight.

Fate (or perhaps the universe) had stepped in with a well-timed, redirection in my lifestyle; coming at a time when I was beginning to question the pros and cons of any future flirtings with the big mountains.

The last decade had indeed bestowed upon me a trove of wild adventures that were both empowering and transforming, but this lifestyle now seemed to be a little frivolous and misdirected, as my passion and focus shifted to raising kids, while also making the first ascents of rock climbs with Julie on some newly discovered wilderness crags near her house.

In the coming months, I relived many of those epic moments, while trying to assess what I might have done to alter the outcomes and summit these mountains. What strategies might I have changed if I could only go back in time?

On many previous trips, foul weather had been the major bail factor, but perhaps unwarranted fear, misguided decisions and poor judgement had also played a part too.

Was I too much of a chicken to really put my life on the line as often as needed?

What strategies might I change if I could only go back in time?

All those long, uncertain years spent as an aspiring climber and just now realizing that being as obsessed as I was, so driven to follow through with all the specific mountaineering goals that I'd conjured up; no matter how farfetched or unattainable; That was a pure blessing in itself.

The love of climbing has always been a guiding light throughout all the darker times, from the very beginning. I recalled my chance encounter with that instructional climbing book so long ago and how I foolishly taught myself to climb. How the unconditional obsession with the sport steered me away from a future life of making bad choices and later, when climbing even steered me back on the right course after the heartache of my first break up.

But what about all those unsettlingly close calls and nearly fatal mishaps? How many serious brushes with death do we need to encounter before throwing in the towel and telling ourselves that it is just not worth it? I have no real clue but having survived a great many of them and lived to tell this tale, I realize that my true love affair with climbing stems from making those risky but inspired judgement calls and spur of the moment decisions that bring about some occasional hard-won successes that keep the flames of obsession burning brightly.

I hope that the preceding narratives were able to recapture some of those enduring and oftentimes life changing moments and imbue the reader with the same passion; to follow her/ his summit or wall bagging dreams to an edge of life, high fiving, bear hugging conclusion.

Hopefully, more often than me.

At the very least, try to learn from, and not replicate some of the mistakes that I made!

THE END.

Tepui basecamp

Sunrise on Apauray Tepui (AKA The Coffin).

Author just before his near drowning incident.

Lower section of the route.

Looking up the route.

Tepui sunrise.

Extreme gardening

Scoping the continuing line after escaping the vulture's lair

Don't fall now

Whew!!

Author hypothermic and thoroughly pissed off after
being deluged on by a waterfall all night.

Bibliography

Jinxed Beyond Reason - Chapter 11.
Formerly -Tales of Climbing and Other Feats of Strength ~ Mountain Freak magazine #5 Summer 1998
and Jinxed ~ Ascent magazine 201, The Vertical Life, 2011
The Vulture's Garden - Chapter 13.
Formerly - The Vulture's Garden, Rock and Ice magazine #189, October 2010
Whimperings -Chapter 8.
Formerly - Wimps ~ The Mountain Yodel magazine, #6, 1997
No Food for Thought ~ Rock and Ice magazine #231, January 2016. (Reference to Ladyfinger).
The Enigmatic Syringe. Chapter 7 ~ Courtesy Steve 'Crusher' Bartlett, author of Desert Rock, by Sharp End Publishing.
La Cueva Del Chupa Cabra - Chapter 9 ~ Mona Ami. A previous article on Mona Island by Craig Luebben in Rock and Ice magazine #76, December 1996

ACKNOWLEDGEMENTS

First and foremost, a great debt of gratitude must be bestowed upon Jerry Rock, a longtime friend and climbing partner who spent endless hours formatting my stories and helping me to unravel the complexities of the publishing process.

A big thank you goes out to my daughter Summer for her invaluable work in designing the book cover.

Finally, to all my great and supportive friends, soul mates, life and climbing partners who are far too numerous to mention, spanning almost thirty years of incredible climbing and travel adventures.

Many thanks and blessings to all.

Cheers,

Strappo Hughes.